BIRDS
ALTERNATIVE NAMES

BIRDS

ALTERNATIVE NAMES

A World Checklist

Walter Lodge

BLANDFORD

To the memory of Meg

Blandford
An imprint of Cassell,
Villiers House, 41/47 Strand, London WC2N 5JE

First published in the United Kingdom in 1991

Distributed in the United States by
Sterling Publishing Co. Inc.
387 Park Avenue South, New York, NY 10016–8810

Distributed in Australia by
Capricorn Link (Australia) Pty Ltd
P.O. Box 665, Lane Cove, NSW 2066

British Library Cataloguing in Publication Data
Lodge, Walter
Birds alternative names.
1. Birds. Names
I. Title
598.014

ISBN 0–7137–2267–3

Typeset by Fakenham Photosetting Ltd, Fakenham, Norfolk
Printed and bound in Great Britain
by Mackays of Chatham

Contents

Introduction 7

Orders, Families and Subfamilies 9

Alternative English Names 15

Appendix 187

Bibliography 195

Index 198

Introduction

This is not a complete list of birds of the world. It is a list of those birds which have one or more alternative names in common usage, but does not include local or dialect names either in Britain or abroad. It does not attempt to deal with the classification of species, nor explain the scientific or English names, but those birds which are listed are in the generally accepted taxonomic order.

Whilst some alternative names, such as the Eurasian Green Plover, Peewit or Lapwing, and the popular Pink, Leadbeater's or Major Mitchell's Cockatoo from Australia are well known, there are a great number of other species with at least one, and sometimes as many as eight, alternative names, some quite diverse, which are not so well known. For example a Pigmy Goose and a Cotton Teal are synonymous, and a Green-tailed Trainbearer is the same Hummingbird as a Little Long-tailed Sylph. A Red-headed Finch is synonymous with a Paradise Sparrow, and a Double-collared Seedeater is the same bird as a Bluish Finch.

Significantly, in his introduction to *A Checklist of Birds of the World*, Edward Gruson states that, 'With regard to the English common names, a pleasant disorder reigns.' He goes on to say, 'In developing this list, alternative names for species were commonly found.' Similarly, Joseph Forshaw, in his preface to *Parrots of the World*, states that, 'The choice of English names has been a difficult problem', and Michael Walters, in *The Complete Birds of the World* refers to the 'Various alternatives available', when selecting English names.

The purpose of this book is to list the many alternative names that the above authors, and others, have had to consider, and which all appear from time to time in various books or articles. When, as sometimes occurs, one of the English names is quoted without a scientific name, it is difficult to know just which species is being referred to, and this may lead to confusion. By reference to this list, it will be simple to identify any given name with its scientific name, and

7

thus with any other name by which the species is known and which may be more familiar.

The sequence of families and genera are given in the accepted taxonomic order, but for simplicity, and for easy reference by the non-professional user, the species within genera are listed alphabetically. There is a precedent for this alphabetical listing in Gruson's *A Checklist of Birds of the World*.

An English name of a subspecies which differs from that of its species is not regarded as an alternative name and so it is not included; but if a subspecies has more than one name then it is included.

Where all, or many, species of a family or genus are known by the same alternative name or names (e.g. the Gaviidae, whose members are all known as either Divers or Loons, and *Lonchura*, many species of which are known as either Mannikins, Munias or Nuns), this is noted at the first reference to the family or genus. If this is the only difference in name, individual species are not listed.

In some cases the same English name is used for more than one species. For example, both *Saxicoloides fulicata* and *Turdus nigriceps* are sometimes referred to as a Black Robin. As both of these species have an alternative name they will both be included in the list. In cases such as *Malimbus rubriceps* and *Quelea erythrops*, where both are known as a Red-headed Weaver, only *Quelea erythrops* has an alternative name and therefore *Malimbus rubriceps* will not be listed. It will, however, be included in the appendix, which consists of all those English names which are used for more than one species, and which have not been dealt with by footnotes, together with their scientific names. All such English names are marked with an asterisk, e.g. Diablotin*. In most cases of an English name being shared by two species, these species are in the same genus and will be readily noticed without need to refer to the appendix.

The names listed are taken from many sources, including numerous field guides and other ornithological literature, avicultural books, journals, magazines and society newsletters, CITES lists, dealers' lists, cigarette and other trade cards, encyclopedias and books of knowledge, and, indeed, from any source where birds are written about or mentioned.

Inevitably some lesser known species with alternative names will have been missed, as no doubt will some lesser-used names for more well-known species, but generally, particularly as far as birds known to aviculture are concerned, all names are included.

Note: s.f. indicates a subfamily.

Orders, Families and Subfamilies

RHEIFORMES	17 **Rheidae**	Rheas
CASUARIIFORMES	17 **Casuariidae**	Cassowaries
APTERYGIFORMES	17 **Apterygidae**	Kiwis
TINAMIFORMES	17 **Tinamidae**	Tinamous
SPHENISCIFORMES	18 **Spheniscidae**	Penguins
GAVIIFORMES	19 **Gaviidae**	Divers (Loons)
PODICIPEDIFORMES	19 **Podicipedidae**	Grebes
PROCELLARIIFORMES	19 **Diomedeidae**	Albatrosses
	19 **Procellariidae**	Shearwaters, Fulmars, Petrels
	21 **Hydrobatidae**	Storm Petrels
PELECANIFORMES	21 **Phaethontidae**	Tropicbirds
	21 **Pelecanidae**	Pelicans
	21 **Sulidae**	Boobies
	21 **Phalacrocoracidae**	Cormorants
	22 **Anhingidae**	Anhingas
CICONIIFORMES	22 **Ardeidae**	Herons, Egrets
	23 **Balaenicipitidae**	Whale-headed Stork
	23 **Scopidae**	Hammerhead Stork
	23 **Ciconiidae**	Storks
	24 **Threskiornithidae**	Ibises, Spoonbills
	24 **Phoenicopteridae**	Flamingos
ANSERIFORMES	24 **Anhimidae**	Screamers
	25 **Anatidae**	Ducks, Geese
FALCONIFORMES	28 **Accipitridae**	Hawks, Old World Vultures, Harriers, Eagles
	31 **Falconidae**	Falcons, Caracaras
GALLIFORMES	32 **Megapodiidae**	Megapodes
	32 **Cracidae**	Curassows, Guans, Chachalacas
	33 **Tetraonidae**	Grouse

9

GALLIFORMES (cont.)	34	**Phasianidae**	Quails, Francolins, Partridges, Pheasants, Peafowl
	38	**Numididae**	Guinea Fowl
	38	**Turnicidae**	Bustard Quails
	39	**Pedionomidae**	Plains Wanderer
GRUIFORMES	39	**Gruidae**	Cranes
	39	**Aramidae**	Limpkin
	40	**Psophiidae**	Trumpeters
	40	**Rallidae**	Rails, Coots, Gallinules
	42	**Cariamidae**	Seriemas
	42	**Otididae**	Bustards
CHARADRIIFORMES	43	**Jacanidae**	Jacanas
	43	**Charadriidae**	Plovers, Dotterels
	44	**Scolopacidae**	Snipe, Sandpipers
	45	**Recurvirostridae**	Avocets, Stilts
	45	**Phalaropodidae**	Phalaropes
	45	**Burhinidae**	Thick-knees
	46	**Glareolidae**	Coursers, Pratincoles
	46	**Thinocoridae**	Seedsnipe
	46	**Stercorariidae**	Skuas, Jaegers
	46	**Laridae**	Gulls, Terns
	47	**Alcidae**	Auks, Murres
COLUMBIFORMES	48	**Pteroclidae**	Sandgrouse
	48	**Columbidae**	Pigeons, Doves
PSITTACIFORMES	58	**Loriidae**	Lories, Lorikeets
	60	**Cacatuidae**	Cockatoos
	62	**Psittacidae**	Parrots, Lovebirds, Macaws
CUCULIFORMES	79	**Musophagidae**	Plantain-eaters, Turacos, Go-Away Birds
	80	**Cuculidae**	Cuckoos, Roadrunners, Coucals
STRIGIFORMES	81	**Tytonidae**	Barn Owls
	82	**Strigidae**	Owls
CAPRIMULGIFORMES	83	**Steatornithidae**	Oilbird
	84	**Caprimulgidae**	Nightjars

APODIFORMES	84	**Apodidae**	Swifts
	85	**Trochilidae**	Hummingbirds
COLIIFORMES	90	**Coliidae**	Mousebirds (Colies)
TROGONIFORMES	90	**Trogonidae**	Trogons
CORACIIFORMES	91	**Alcedinidae**	Kingfishers
	93	**Todidae**	Todies
	93	**Momotidae**	Motmots
	93	**Meropidae**	Bee-eaters
	93	**Leptosomatidae**	Courol
	93	**Coraciidae**	Rollers
	94	**Phoeniculidae**	Wood Hoopoes
	94	**Bucerotidae**	Hornbills
PICIFORMES	95	**Galbulidae**	Jacamars
	95	**Capitonidae**	Barbets
	97	**Indicatoridae**	Honeyguides
	97	**Ramphastidae**	Toucans
	99	**Picidae**	Woodpeckers, Piculets
PASSERIFORMES	101	**Eurylaimidae**	Broadbills
	102	**Dendrocolaptidae**	Wood-creepers
	102	**Furnariidae**	Ovenbirds
	103	**Formicariidae**	Antbirds
	104	**Pittidae**	Pittas
	105	**Tyrannidae**	Tyrant Flycatchers
	108	**Pipridae**	Manakins
	108	**Cotingidae**	Cotingas, Cocks-of-the-Rock, Becards
	110	**Menuridae**	Lyrebirds
	110	**Atrichornithidae**	Scrub-birds
	110	**Alaudidae**	Larks
	111	**Hirundinidae**	Swallows, Martins
	112	**Motacillidae**	Wagtails, Pipits
	113	**Campephagidae**	Cuckoo Shrikes
	114	**Pycnonotidae**	Bulbuls
	117	**Irenidae**	Leafbirds
	118	**Prionopidae**	Helmet Shrikes
	118	**Laniidae**	Shrikes
	119	**Vangidae**	Vanga Shrikes
	119	**Ptilogonatidae**	Waxwings
	119	**Cinclidae**	Dippers
	119	**Troglodytidae**	Wrens

PASSERIFORMES (cont.)	120	**Mimidae**	Mockingbirds, Thrashers
	120	**Prunellidae**	Accentors
		Muscicapidae	
	120	*Turdinae*	Thrushes, Wren Thrushes
	124	*Timaliinae*	Babblers, Wren Tits
	131	*Paradoxorni-thinae*	Parrotbills
	132	*Sylviinae*	Old World Warblers
	135	*Malurinae*	Wren Warblers
	136	*Acanthizinae*	Australasian Warblers
	136	*Muscicapinae*	Old World Flycatchers
	138	*Rhipidurinae*	Fantail Flycatchers
	138	*Monarchinae*	Monarch Flycatchers
	139	*Pachycephalinae*	Whistlers, Shrike Thrushes
	139	**Aegithalidae**	Long-tailed Tits
	140	**Remizidae**	Penduline Tits
	140	**Paridae**	Tits, Titmice, Chickadees
	141	**Sittidae**	Nuthatches
	141	**Dicaeidae**	Flower-peckers
	142	**Nectariniidae**	Sunbirds
	144	**Zosteropidae**	White-eyes
	145	**Meliphagidae**	Honey-eaters
		Emberizidae	
	146	*Emberizinae*	Buntings, American Sparrows
	150	*Catamblyrhyn-chinae*	Plush-capped Finch
	151	*Cardinalinae*	Cardinal-Grosbeaks
	152	*Thraupinae*	Tanagers, Honeycreepers
	156	**Icteridae**	Blackbirds, Troupials

PASSERIFORMES (cont.)

Fringillidae

158	*Fringillinae*	Chaffinches, Brambling
158	*Carduelinae*	Goldfinches and allied Finches
162	**Estrildidae**	Waxbills

Ploceidae

172	*Viduinae*	Parasitic Whydahs
172	*Ploceinae*	Weavers, Sparrows
177	**Sturnidae**	Starlings
181	**Oriolidae**	Old World Orioles
181	**Dicruridae**	Drongos
182	**Cracticidae**	Butcherbirds
182	**Ptilonorhynchidae**	Bowerbirds
182	**Paradisaeidae**	Birds of Paradise
184	**Corvidae**	Crows, Magpies, Jays, Ravens

Alternative English Names

FAMILY/GENUS	SPECIES/SUBSPECIES	ENGLISH NAMES

Rheidae Rheas

Rhea	*americana*	Greater Rhea
		Common Rhea
		Rhea
Pterocnemia	*pennata*	Lesser Rhea
		Darwin's Rhea
		Puna Rhea

Casuariidae Cassowaries

Casuarius	*bennetti*	Dwarf Cassowary
		Bennett's Cassowary
	casuarius	Australian Cassowary
		Double-wattled Cassowary
		Two-wattled Cassowary
	unappendiculatus	Single-wattled Cassowary
		One-wattled Cassowary

Apterygidae Kiwis

Apteryx	*australis*	Brown Kiwi
		Common Kiwi
	oweni	Little Spotted Kiwi
		Little Grey Kiwi

Tinamidae Tinamous

Tinamus	*tao*	Grey Tinamou
		Great Grey Tinamou
Nothocercus	*bonapartei*	Highland Tinamou
		Bonaparte's Tinamou
	julius	Tawny-breasted Tinamou
		Verreaux's Tinamou
Crypturellus	*boucardi*	Slaty-breasted Tinamou
		Boucard's Tinamou
	brevirostris	Rusty Tinamou
		Short-billed Tinamou
	casiquiare	Barred Tinamou
		Casiquiare Tinamou
	cinnamomeus	Rufescent Tinamou
		Cinnamon Tinamou
	duidae	Grey-legged Tinamou
		Duida Tinamou
	kerriae	Choco Tinamou
		Kerr's Tinamou

17

Tinamidae Tinamous (cont.)

	soui	Little Tinamou
		Pileated Tinamou
	transfasciatus	Pale-browed Tinamou
		Steere's Tinamou
Rhynchotus	*rufescens*	Red-winged Tinamou
		Rufous Tinamou

(All species of genus *Nothura* alternatively known as Nothuras or Tinamous.)

Nothura	*boraquira*	White-bellied Nothura
		Marbled Nothura
	minor	Lesser Nothura
		Least Nothura
Eudromia	*elegans*	Elegant Crested Tinamou
		Elegant Tinamou
	formosa	Quebracho Crested Tinamou
		Quebracho Tinamou
		Quebracho
Tinamotis	*ingoufi*	Patagonian Tinamou
		Ingouf's Tinamou
	pentlandii	Puna Tinamou
		Pentland's Tinamou

Spheniscidae Penguins

Pygoscelis	*antarctica*	Chinstrap Penguin
		Bearded Penguin
Eudyptes	*sclateri*	Erect-crested Penguin
		Big-crested Penguin
Megadyptes	*antipodes*	Yellow-eyed Penguin
		Yellow-crowned Penguin
Eudyptula	*minor*	Little Blue Penguin
		Little Penguin
		Blue Penguin
		Fairy Penguin
Spheniscus	*demersus*	Jackass Penguin
		Black-footed Penguin
		Cape Penguin
	humboldti	Humboldt Penguin
		Peruvian Penguin

Gaviidae Divers
(All species alternatively known as Divers or Loons.)

Gavia	*adamsii*	Yellow-billed Loon
		White-billed Diver
	arctica	Arctic Loon
		Black-throated Diver
	immer	Common Loon
		Great Northern Diver

Podicipedidae Grebes

Podiceps	*auritus*	Horned Grebe
		Slavonian Grebe
	dominicus	Least Grebe
		Mexican Grebe
	nigricollis	Black-necked Grebe
		Eared Grebe
	novaehollandiae	Black-throated Little Grebe
		Black-throated Grebe
		Australian Dabchick
	rolland	White-tufted Grebe
		Rolland's Grebe
		Rolland's Golden Grebe
	ruficollis	Little Grebe
		Dabchick
	rufolaratus	Delacour's Little Grebe
		Alaotra Grebe
Podilymbus	*gigas*	Atitlan Grebe
		Giant Pied-billed Grebe

Diomedeidae Albatrosses

Diomedea	*albatrus*	Short-tailed Albatross
		Steller's Albatross
	cauta	White-capped Albatross
		Shy Albatross
	irrorata	Galapagos Albatross
		Waved Albatross

Procellariidae Shearwaters, Fulmars, Petrels

Macronectes	*giganteus*	Giant Fulmar
		Giant Petrel
Daption	*capensis*	Cape Petrel

Procellariidae Shearwaters, Fulmars, Petrels (cont.)

FAMILY/GENUS	SPECIES/SUBSPECIES	ENGLISH NAMES
		Cape Pigeon
		Pintado
		Pintado Petrel
Fulmarus	*glacialoides*	Silver-grey Fulmar
		Silver-grey Petrel
		Southern Fulmar
		Antarctic Fulmar
Pachyptila	*belcheri*	Slender-billed Prion
		Narrow-billed Prion
	desolata	Dove Prion
		Antarctic Prion
Adamstor	*cinereus*	Grey Petrel
		Brown Petrel
Procellaria	*parkinsoni*	Parkinson's Petrel
		Black Petrel
Puffinus	*assimilis*	Little Shearwater
		Allied Shearwater
	bulleri	Grey-backed Shearwater
		Buller's Shearwater
		New Zealand Shearwater
	carneipes	Flesh-footed Shearwater
		Pale-footed Shearwater
	leucomelas	White-faced Shearwater
		Streaked Shearwater
	nativitatis	Black Shearwater
		Christmas Shearwater
	tenuirostris	Short-tailed Shearwater
		Slender-billed Shearwater
Pterodroma	*cahow*	Bermuda Petrel
		Cahow
	hasitata	Black-capped Petrel
		Capped Petrel
		Diablotin★
	incerta	Hooded Petrel
		Atlantic Petrel
		Schlegel's Petrel
	inexpectata	Scaled Petrel
		Mottled Petrel
		Peale's Petrel
	leucoptera	Stout-billed Gadfly Petrel

		Collared Petrel
		Gould's Petrel
	macroptera	Grey-faced Petrel
		Great-winged Petrel

Hydrobatidae Storm Petrels

Pelagodroma	*marina*	White-faced Storm Petrel
		Frigate Petrel
Oceanodroma	*castro*	Harcourt's Storm Petrel
		Madeiran Storm Petrel
		Madeiran Fork-tailed Petrel
	leucorhoa	Leach's Storm Petrel
		Leach's Fork-tailed Petrel

Phaethontidae Tropicbirds

Phaethon	*lepturus*	White-tailed Tropicbird
		Yellow-billed Tropicbird

Pelecanidae Pelicans

Pelecanus	*philippensis*	Spot-billed Pelican
		Grey Pelican

Sulidae Boobies

Sula	*dactylatra*	Blue-faced Booby
		Masked Booby
	variegata	Peruvian Booby
		Variegated Booby

Phalacrocoracidae Cormorants
(Many species alternatively known as Cormorants or Shags.)

Phalacrocorax	*africanus*	Reed Cormorant
		Long-tailed Cormorant
	albiventer	King Cormorant
		MacQuarie Island Shag
	aristotelis	Shag
		Green Cormorant
	atriceps	Blue-eyed Cormorant
		Imperial Cormorant
	capillatus	Temminck's Cormorant
		Japanese Cormorant
	carbo	Great Cormorant

Phalacrocoracidae Cormorants (cont.)

		Cormorant
		White-breasted Cormorant
		Black Shag
	carunculatus	New Zealand King Shag
		Rough-faced Cormorant
	magellanicus	Rock Cormorant
		Magellan Cormorant
	niger	Pygmy Cormorant
		Javanese Cormorant
	olivaceus	Neotropic Cormorant
		Mexican Cormorant
		Olivaceous Cormorant
		Bigua
		Bigua Cormorant

Anhingidae Anhingas
(All species alternatively known as Anhingas, Darters or Snakebirds.)

Ardeidae Herons, Egrets

Ardea	*novaehollandiae*	White-faced Heron
		White-fronted Heron
		Blue Crane*
	pacifica	White-necked Heron
		Pacific Heron
Butorides	*striatus*	Striated Heron
		Green-backed Heron
		Little Green Heron
Bubulcus	*ibis*	Cattle Egret
		Buff-backed Heron
Egretta	*alba*	Great Egret
		Great White Egret
		White Egret
		Great White Heron
		White Heron
		American Egret
		Large Egret
		Common Egret
	ardesiaca	Black Heron
		Black Egret
	intermedia	Intermediate Heron

		Plumed Egret
		Yellow-billed Egret
	sacra	Eastern Reef Heron
		Blue Reef Heron
		Blue Crane★
	tricolor	Louisiana Heron
		Tri-coloured Heron
Nycticorax	*caledonicus*	Rufous Night Heron
		Nankeen Night Heron
	nycticorax	Black-crowned Night Heron
		Black-capped Night Heron
Ixobrychus	*sinensis*	Chinese Little Bittern
		Yellow Bittern
	sturmii	Dwarf Bittern
		Rail Heron

Balaenicipitidae Whale-headed Stork

Balaeniceps	*rex*	Whale-headed Stork
		Whalehead
		Shoebill
		Shoe-billed Stork

Scopidae Hammerhead Stork

Scopus	*umbretta*	Hammerhead Stork
		Hammerkop
		Hamerkop

Ciconiidae Storks

Mycteria	*americana*	Wood Stork
		Wood Ibis★
Ibis	*ibis*	Yellow-billed Stork
		African Wood Stork
		Wood Ibis★
	leucocephalus	Painted Stork
		White-headed Stork
		Asian Wood Ibis
Ciconia	*abdimii*	White-bellied Stork
		Abdim's Stork
	ciconia boyciana	Japanese White Stork
		White Oriental Stork
	episcopus	White-necked Stork

23

Ciconiidae Storks (cont.)

		Woolly-necked Stork
		Bishop Stork
Jabiru	*mycteria*	Jabiru
		Black-necked Stork
Leptoptilos	*dubius*	Greater Adjutant Stork
		Adjutant Stork
	javanicus	Lesser Adjutant Stork
		Javan Adjutant Stork
		Hair-crested Stork

Threskiornithidae Ibises, Spoonbills

Threskiornis	*aethiopica*	Sacred Ibis
		Sand Ibis
	melanocephala	Oriental Ibis
		Black-headed Ibis
		Asian White Ibis
Geronticus	*eremita*	Hermit Ibis
		Bald Ibis
		Northern Bald Ibis
		Waldrap
Platalea	*regia*	Royal Spoonbill
		Black-billed Spoonbill

Phoenicopteridae Flamingos

Phoenicopterus	*ruber*	Greater Flamingo
		Roseate Flamingo
		Rosy Flamingo
		Scarlet Flamingo
		American Flamingo
		Caribbean Flamingo
		Cuban Flamingo
		West Indian Flamingo

Anhimidae Screamers

Chauna	*chavaria*	Northern Screamer
		Black-necked Screamer
	torquata	Southern Screamer
		Crested Screamer

Anatidae Ducks, Geese

(All species of genus *Dendrocygna* alternatively known as Tree Ducks or Whistling Ducks.)

FAMILY/GENUS	SPECIES/SUBSPECIES	ENGLISH NAMES
Dendrocygna	*arborea*	West Indian Tree Duck
		Cuban Tree Duck
		Black-billed Tree Duck
	arcuata	Whistling Tree Duck
		Wandering Tree Duck
		Water Whistling Duck
		Water Whistle Duck
	autumnalis	Black-bellied Tree Duck
		Red-billed Tree Duck
	eytoni	Plumed Whistling Duck
		Eyton's Tree Duck
		Grass Whistling Duck
		Grass Whistle Duck
	javanica	Lesser Whistling Duck
		Javan Tree Duck
		Indian Whistling Duck
Anser	*cygnoides*	Swan Goose
		Chinese Goose
Branta	*bernicla*	Brant
		Brent Goose
	sandvicensis	Hawaiian Goose
		Néné
Cereopsis	*novaehollandiae*	Cape Barren Goose
		Cereopsis Goose
Chloephaga	*picta*	Upland Goose
		Magellan Goose
		Lesser Magellan Goose
Cyanochen	*cyanoptera*	Blue-winged Goose
		Abyssinian Goose
Tadorna	*cana*	African Shelduck
		Cape Shelduck
	ferruginea	Ruddy Shelduck
		Brahminy Duck
	radjah	White-headed Shelduck
		Radjah Shelduck
		Black-backed Shelduck
		Burdekin Duck
		Burdekin Shelduck

Anatidae Ducks, Geese (cont.)

	tadornoides	Mountain Duck
		Australian Shelduck
	variegata	Paradise Duck
		Paradise Shelduck
		New Zealand Shelduck
Anas	*americana*	American Wigeon
		Baldpate
	auklandica nesiotis	Flightless Teal
		Campbell Island Brown Teal
	bahamensis	White-cheeked Pintail
		Lesser Bahama Pintail
	capensis	Cape Wigeon
		African Cape Teal
		Cape Teal
		Pink-billed Duck
	castanea	Chestnut Teal
		Brown Teal
	erythrorhyncha	Red-billed Duck
		Red-billed Teal
		Red-billed Pintail
	flavirostris	Speckled Teal
		Chilean Teal
		South American Green-winged Teal
	formosa	Baikal Teal
		Spectacled Teal
	georgica	Yellow-billed Pintail
		Chilean Pintail
		Brown Pintail
	oustaleti	Oustalet's Grey Duck
		Marianas Grey Duck
		Marianas Mallard
	rhynchotis	Blue-winged Shoveler
		Australian Shoveler
	sibilatrix	Southern Wigeon
		Chiloe Wigeon
	smithii	Smith's Shoveler
		Cape Shoveler
	sparsa	African Black Duck
		Black River Duck
	specularis	Spectacled Duck

FAMILY/GENUS	SPECIES/SUBSPECIES	ENGLISH NAMES
		Bronze-winged Duck
	superciliosa	Australian Grey Duck
		Australian Black Duck
		Pacific Black Duck
	versicolor	Silver Teal
		Versicolour Teal
Polysticta	*stelleri*	Steller's Eider
		Little Eider
		Siberian Eider
Somateria	*fischeri*	Spectacled Eider
		Fischer's Eider
Aythya	*australis*	Australian Pochard
		Australian White-eye
		Hardhead
	baeri	Baer's Pochard
		Eastern White-eyed Pochard
	marila	Greater Scaup
		Scaup
	nyroca	White-eyed Pochard
		Ferruginous White-eye
		Ferruginous Duck
Netta	*erythrophthalma*	
	erythrophthalma	Southern Pochard
		South American Pochard
		Red-eyed Pochard
	e. brunnea	African Pochard
		South African Pochard
	rufina	Red-crested Pochard
		Red-crested Duck
Chenonetta	*jubata*	Maned Goose
		Maned Wood Duck
		Australian Wood Duck
Amazonetta	*brasiliensis*	Brazilian Duck
		Greater Brazilian Duck
Aix	*sponsa*	Wood Duck
		Carolina Duck
Nettapus	*auritus*	African Pygmy Goose
		Dwarf Goose
	coromandelianus	Cotton Pygmy Goose
		Pygmy Goose
		Cotton Teal

FAMILY/GENUS	SPECIES/SUBSPECIES	ENGLISH NAMES

Anatidae Ducks, Geese (cont.)

Sarkidiornis	*melanotos*	Knob-billed Goose
		Knob-billed Duck
		Black-backed Goose
		Comb Duck
		Nakta
		Nukta
Pteronetta	*hartlaubii*	Hartlaub's Goose
		Hartlaub's Duck
Melanitta	*nigra*	Black Scoter
		Common Scoter
Clangula	*hyemalis*	Oldsquaw
		Long-tailed Duck
Mergus	*albellus*	Smew
		Smee
		White Nun
	merganser	Common Merganser
		Goosander

Accipitridae Hawks, Old World Vultures, Harriers, Eagles

Aviceda	*jerdoni*	Brown-crested Lizard Hawk
		Jerdon's Baza
	leuphotes	Black-crested Lizard Hawk
		Black Baza
	subcristata	Crested Lizard Hawk
		Crested Baza
Pernis	*ptilorhynchus*	Crested Honey Buzzard
		Asiatic Honey Buzzard
Elanus	*caeruleus*	Black-winged Kite
		Black-shouldered Kite*
Rostrhamus	*sociabilis*	Snail Kite
		Everglades Kite
Milvus	*migrans*	Black Kite
		Pariah Kite
Haliaeetus	*leucoryphus*	Pallas's Sea Eagle
		Pallas's Fish Eagle
	vocifer	African Fish Eagle
		West African River Eagle
		River Eagle
Ichthyophaga	*ichthyaetus*	Grey-headed Fishing Eagle
		Greater Fishing Eagle

FAMILY/GENUS	SPECIES/SUBSPECIES	ENGLISH NAMES
Gypohierax	*angolensis*	Palm-nut Vulture
		Vulturine Fish Eagle
		Eagle Vulture
Neophron	*percnopterus*	Egyptian Vulture
		Scavenger Vulture
Gypaetus	*barbatus*	Bearded Vulture
		Lammergeier
Sarcogyps	*calvus*	Indian Black Vulture
		Pondicherry Vulture
		King Vulture★
Aegypius	*tracheliotus*	Lappet-faced Vulture
		Nubian Vulture
Circaetus	*cinerascens*	Smaller Banded Snake Eagle
		Western Banded Snake Eagle
	cinereus	Snake Eagle★
		Brown Harrier
		Brown Harrier Eagle
		Brown Snake Eagle
	gallicus	Short-toed Eagle
		Snake Eagle★
		Black-breasted Snake Eagle
		Serpent Eagle
Polyboroides	*radiatus*	African Harrier-Hawk
		Gymnogene
Circus	*aeruginosus*	Marsh Harrier
		Swamp Hawk
	cyaneus	Marsh Hawk
		Hen Harrier
Melierax	*metabates*	Chanting Goshawk
		Dark Chanting Goshawk
Accipiter	*badius*	Shikra
		Little Banded Goshawk
	castanilius	Chestnut-flanked Goshawk
		Chestnut-bellied Goshawk
	fasciatus	Brown Goshawk
		Australian Goshawk
	haplochrous	White-bellied Hawk
		New Caledonian Sparrowhawk
	melanoleucus	Great Sparrowhawk
		Black Sparrowhawk
		Black Goshawk

Accipitridae Hawks, Old World Vultures, Harriers, Eagles (cont.)

	rufiventris	Rufous-breasted Sparrowhawk
		Red-breasted Sparrowhawk
	soloensis	Chinese Sparrowhawk
		Grey Frog Hawk
	toussenelii	Vinous-chested Goshawk
		West African Goshawk
Busarellus	*nigricollis*	Black-collared Hawk
		Fishing Buzzard
Parabuteo	*unicinctus*	Harris's Hawk
		Bay-winged Hawk
Buteo	*albicaudatus*	White-tailed Hawk
		White-breasted Buzzard
	buteo	Common Buzzard
		Buzzard
		Steppe Buzzard
	lagopus	Rough-legged Hawk
		Rough-legged Buzzard
	leucorrhous	White-rumped Hawk
		Rufous-thighed Hawk
	magnirostris	Roadside Hawk
		Insect Hawk
		Large-billed Hawk
	oreophilus	Mountain Buzzard
		Forest Buzzard
	poecilochrous	Variable Hawk★
		Gurney's Buzzard
	polyosoma	Red-backed Hawk
		Variable Hawk★
Harpyopsis	*novaeguineae*	New Guinea Harpy Eagle
		Harpy-like Eagle
Aquila	*rapax*	Tawny Eagle
		Steppe Eagle
	verreauxii	Verreaux's Eagle
		Black Eagle
Hieraaetus	*kienerii*	Rufous-bellied Hawk Eagle
		Chestnut-bellied Hawk Eagle
Spizaetus	*cirrhatus*	Crested Hawk Eagle
		Changeable Hawk Eagle
	nanus	Small Hawk Eagle
		Wallace's Hawk Eagle

FAMILY/GENUS	SPECIES/SUBSPECIES	ENGLISH NAMES
	nipalensis	Hodgson's Hawk Eagle
		Mountain Hawk Eagle
		Feather-toed Hawk Eagle
Oroaetus	*isidori*	Black and Chestnut Eagle
		Isidor's Eagle

Falconidae   Falcons, Caracaras

Daptrius	*ater*	Black Caracara
		Yellow-throated Caracara
Phalcoboenus	*albogularis*	White-throated Caracara
		Darwin's Caracara
	australis	Striated Caracara
		Forster's Caracara
		Falkland Island Caracara
		Johnny Rook
Polyborus	*plancus*	Crested Caracara
		Common Caracara
		Audubon's Caracara
Micrastur	*buckleyi*	Buckley's Forest Falcon
		Traylor's Forest Falcon
	plumbeus	Plumbeous Forest Falcon
		Sclater's Forest Falcon
Microhierax	*caerulescens*	Red-thighed Falconet
		Bornean Falconet

(Many species of genus *Falco* alternatively known as Kestrels or Falcons.)

Falco	*cenchroides*	Nankeen Kestrel
		Australian Kestrel
	chicquera	Red-headed Falcon
		Red-necked Falcon
		Red-headed Merlin
	columbarius	Merlin
		Pigeon Hawk
	kreyenborgi	Pallid Falcon
		Kleinschmidt's Falcon
	longipennis	Little Falcon
		Australian Hobby
	moluccensis	Spotted Kestrel
		Moluccan Kestrel
	rupicoloides	Greater Kestrel
		White-eyed Kestrel
	sparverius	American Kestrel

Falconidae Falcons, Caracaras (cont.)

		American Sparrowhawk
	zoniventris	Madagascar Banded Kestrel
		Barred Kestrel

Megapodiidae   Megapodes
(All species alternatively known as Megapodes, Scrub Fowl or Scrub Hens.)

Megapodius	*pritchardii*	Polynesian Scrub Hen
		Pritchard's Scrub Fowl
		Malau Fowl

Cracidae   Curassows, Guans, Chachalacas

Ortalis	*erythroptera*	Rufous-headed Chachalaca
		Ecuadorian Chachalaca
	garrula	Chestnut-winged Chachalaca
		Chattering Guan
	ruficauda	Rufous-vented Chachalaca
		Red-tailed Guan
	motmot	Little Chachalaca
		Variable Chachalaca
	vetula	Plain Chachalaca
		Common Chachalaca
Penelope	*jacucaca*	White-browed Guan
		Brown Guan
	obscura	Dusky-legged Guan
		Dusky Guan
	ortoni	Baudo Guan
		Orton's Guan
	superciliarus	Rusty-margined Guan
		Superciliated Guan
Aburria	*jacutinga*	Black-fronted Piping Guan
		Black-fronted Piping Curassow
		Black-faced Piping Guan
		Black-faced Piping Curassow
	pipile	Common Piping Guan
		Common Piping Curassow
		White-headed Piping Guan
		White-headed Piping Curassow
Chamaepetes	*goudotii*	Sickle-winged Guan
		Goudot's Guan
Penelopina	*nigra*	Black Chachalaca

FAMILY/GENUS	SPECIES/SUBSPECIES	ENGLISH NAMES
		Highland Guan
Oreophasis	*derbianus*	Horned Guan
		Derby Mountain Guan
		Earl of Derby's Mountain Pheasant
Nothocrax	*urumutum*	Nocturnal Curassow
		Nocturnal Guan
Crax	*alberti*	Blue-billed Curassow
		Albert's Curassow
	alector	Black Curassow
		Crested Curassow
	daubentoni	Yellow-knobbed Curassow
		Yellow-billed Curassow
		Daubenton's Curassow
	fasciolata	Bare-faced Curassow
		Sclater's Curassow
	mitu	Razor-billed Curassow
		Greater Razor-billed Curassow
	rubra	Great Curassow
		Mexican Curassow
	tomentosa	Lesser Razor-billed Curassow
		Crestless Curassow

Tetraonidae	Grouse	
Lyrurus	*mlokosiewiczi*	Caucasian Blackcock
		Caucasian Black Grouse
		Caucasian Grouse
	tetrix	Black Grouse
		Blackcock/Greyhen
Lagopus	*lagopus*	Willow Ptarmigan
		Willow Grouse
	mutus	Rock Ptarmigan
		Ptarmigan
Dendrogapus	*falcipennis*	Siberian Spruce Grouse
		Sickle-winged Grouse
	obscurus	Blue Grouse
		Dusky Grouse
		Grey Grouse
Tetrastes	*bonasia*	Hazel Grouse
		Hazelhen

Phasianidae   Quails, Francolins, Partridges, Pheasants, Peafowl

Oreortyx	*pictus*	Mountain Quail
		Painted Quail
		Plumed Quail
		Mountain Partridge
Callipepla	*squamata*	Scaled Quail
		Blue Scaled Quail
		Blue Quail★
		Scaley Colin
		Mexican Quail
		Cottontop Quail
Lophortyx	*californicus*	California Quail
		Valley Quail
		Crested Quail
		Topknot Quail
	douglasii	Elegant Quail
		Douglas Quail
		Benson Quail
		Yaqui Quail
	gambelii	Gambel's Quail
		Desert Quail
Philortyx	*fasciatus*	Banded Quail
		Barred Quail
		Chorunda
Colinus	*cristatus*	Crested Bobwhite
		Crested Quail
	nigrogularis	Black-throated Bobwhite
		Black-throated Quail
		Yuccatan Bobwhite
	virginianus	Bobwhite
		Bobwhite Quail
		Virginian Quail
		Virginian Colin
Odontophorus	*capueira*	Spot-winged Wood Quail
		Capueira Quail
	dialeucos	Black-crowned Wood Quail
		Tacarcuna Wood Quail
	erythrops	Rufous-fronted Wood Quail
		Paramba Quail
	leucolaemus	White-throated Wood Quail
		Black-breasted Quail

34

FAMILY/GENUS	SPECIES/SUBSPECIES	ENGLISH NAMES
Dactylortyx	*thoracicus*	Singing Quail
		Long-toed Partridge
Cyrtonyx	*montezumae mearnsi*	Mearn's Quail
		Harlequin Quail★
		Black Quail
Rhynchortyx	*cinctus*	Tawny-faced Quail
		Long-legged Colin
		Banded Quail★
Tetraophasis	*obscurus*	Verreaux's Monal Partridge
		Verreaux's Pheasant Grouse
	szechenyii	Szechenyi's Monal Partridge
		Szechenyi's Pheasant Grouse
Alectoris	*philbyi*	Philby's Rock Partridge
		Philby's Partridge
		Black-throated Chukar
	magna	Przevalski's Rock Partridge
		Przevalski's Partridge
		Large Rock Partridge
		Great Partridge
	melanocephala	Arabian Chukar
		Rüppell's Partridge
	rufa	Red-legged Partridge
		French Partridge
Francolinus	*afer*	Bare-throated Francolin
		Grey-winged Francolin★
		Red-necked Francolin
	francolinus	Black Francolin
		Black Partridge
	gularis	Swamp Francolin
		Swamp Partridge
	icterorhynchus	Yellow-billed Francolin
		Heuglin's Francolin
	jacksoni	Jackson's Francolin
		Kenya Francolin
	lathami	Latham's Francolin
		Forest Francolin
	levalliantoides	Archer's Greywing
		Orange River Francolin
	nobilis	Ruanda Francolin
		Handsome Francolin
	ochrogaster	Pale-bellied Francolin

Phasianidae Quails, Francolins, Partridges, Pheasants, Peafowl (cont.)

		Tadjouri Francolin
	pictus	Painted Partridge
		Painted Francolin*
	pintadeanus	Chinese Francolin
		Burmese Francolin
	psilolaemus	Montane Francolin
		Relict Francolin
	rufopictus	Painted Francolin*
		Grey-breasted Francolin
	swainsonii	Swainson's Francolin
		Swainson's Spurfowl
Perdix	*dauuricae*	Daurian Partridge
		Bearded Partridge
	perdix	Grey Partridge
		Partridge
		English Partridge
		Hungarian Partridge
		Common Partridge
Coturnix	*chinensis*	Chinese Painted Quail
		Blue-breasted Quail
		King Quail
		Painted Quail
	coromandelica	Black-breasted Quail
		Rain Quail
	coturnix	Common Quail
		Quail
		Migratory Quail
	pectoralis	Pectoral Quail
		Stubble Quail

(Some species of genus *Arborophila* alternatively known as Hill Partridges or Tree Partridges and both of these are also known as Partridges.)

Arborophila	*ardens*	Hainan Hill Partridge
		White-eared Partridge
	brunneopectus	Brown-breasted Hill Partridge
		Bar-backed Hill Partridge
		Bare-throated Tree Partridge*
	cambodiana	Chestnut-headed Tree Partridge
		Cambodian Hill Partridge
	charltonii	Chestnut-breasted Tree Partridge
		Scaly-breasted Partridge

36

FAMILY/GENUS	SPECIES/SUBSPECIES	ENGLISH NAMES
		Eyton's Partridge
		Yellow-legged Partridge
		Green-legged Partridge
	crudigularis	Formosan Hill Partridge
		White-throated Hill Partridge
		Swinhoe's Hill Partridge
	davidi	David's Tree Partridge
		Orange-necked Partridge
	javanica	Chestnut-bellied Tree Partridge
		Javan Hill Partridge
		Bare-throated Tree Partridge★
	mandellii	Red-breasted Hill Partridge
		Mandell's Hill Partridge
	orientalis	Sumatran Hill Partridge
		Horsfield's Tree Partridge
		Campbell's Tree Partridge
	torqueola	Common Hill Partridge
		Necklaced Hill Partridge
		Peora
Rollulus	*roulroul*	Crested Wood Partridge
		Roulroul
		Roulroul Partridge
Bambusicola	*fytchii*	Bamboo Partridge
		Assam Bamboo Partridge
		Indian Bamboo Partridge
		Mountain Bamboo Partridge
		Fytch's Bamboo Partridge
		Anderson's Bamboo Partridge
Tragopan	*temminckii*	Temminck's Tragopan
		Chinese Tragopan
Lophophorus	*impejanus*	Himalayan Monal
		Impeyan Pheasant
Crossoptilon	*crossoptilon*	White Eared Pheasant
		Tibetan Eared Pheasant
	c. harmani	Elwes's Eared Pheasant
		Harman's Eared Pheasant
	mantchuricum	Brown Eared Pheasant
		Hoki
Lophura	*leucomelana lathami*	Horsfield's Kalij
		Black-breasted Kalij

Phasianidae Quails, Francolins, Partridges, Pheasants, Peafowl (cont.)

Gallus	*sonneratii*	Grey Junglefowl
		Sonnerat's Junglefowl
Syrmaticus	*humiae*	Mrs Hume's Pheasant
		Hume's Pheasant
		Hume's Bar-tailed Pheasant
Polyplectron	*bicalcaratum*	Peacock Pheasant
		Common Peacock Pheasant
		Grey Peacock Pheasant
	inopinatum	Rothschild's Peacock Pheasant
		Mountain Peacock Pheasant
Rheinardia	*ocellata*	Crested Argus
		Rheinart's Crested Argus
Afropavo	*congensis*	Congo Peafowl
		African Peafowl

Numididae   Guinea Fowl

Numida	*meleagris*	Helmet Guinea Fowl
		Helmeted Guinea Fowl
		Tufted Guinea Fowl

Turnicidae   Bustard Quails

(Most species alternatively known as Bustard Quails, Button Quails or Hemipodes.)

Turnix	*hottentotta*	Hottentot Button Quail
		Black-rumped Button Quail
	maculosa	Red-backed Button Quail
		Australian Hemipode
	pyrrhothorax	Red-chested Button Quail
		Australian Button Quail
	suscitator	Bustard Quail
		Barred Button Quail
	sylvatica	Little Button Quail*
		Striped Button Quail
		Common Button Quail
		Kurrichane Button Quail
		Andalusian Hemipode
	velox	Little Quail
		Little Button Quail*

FAMILY/GENUS	SPECIES/SUBSPECIES	ENGLISH NAMES

Pedionomidae Plains Wanderer

Pedionomus   *torquatus*   Plains Wanderer
Collared Hemipode

Gruidae Cranes

Grus   *grus*   Crane
Eurasian Crane
Grey Crane

japonensis   Japanese Crane
Manchurian Crane
Red-crowned Crane

leucogeranus   Siberian White Crane
Siberian Crane
Asiatic White Crane
Great White Crane
Snow Crane

nigricollis   Black-necked Crane
Tibetan Crane

vipio   White-naped Crane
White-necked Crane

Anthropoides   *paradisea*   Blue Crane*
Stanley Crane
Paradise Crane

Balearica   *pavonina pavonina*   Crowned Crane
Crested Crane
Balearic Crane
Black-necked Crowned Crane
Dark Crowned Crane
West African Crowned Crane

p. regulorum   South African Crowned Crane
Blue-necked Crowned Crane
Grey-necked Crowned Crane
Cape Crowned Crane

Aramidae Limpkin

Aramus   *guarauna*   Limpkin
Courlon
Great Courlon

39

Psophiidae Trumpeters

Psophia	*crepitans*	Grey-winged Trumpeter
		Common Trumpeter
		Golden-breasted Trumpeter
		Agami
	leucoptera	Pale-winged Trumpeter
		White-winged Trumpeter
	viridis	Dark-winged Trumpeter
		Green-winged Trumpeter

Rallidae Rails, Coots, Gallinules

(Most species of Rail and Crake alternatively known by either name.)

Rallus	*caerulescens*	Kaffir Rail
		African Water Rail
	pectoralis	Lewin's Water Rail
		Auckland Island Rail
	philippensis	Banded Land Rail
		Buff-banded Rail
		Banded Rail
	striatus	Blue-breasted Banded Rail
		Blue-breasted Rail
		Slaty-breasted Rail
	wetmorei	Plain-flanked Rail
		Wetmore's Rail
Tricholimnas	*sylvestris*	Lord Howe Wood Rail
		Wood Hen
Rallina	*eurizonoides*	Banded Crake
		Slaty-legged Banded Rail
		Slaty-legged Crake
	fasciata	Red-legged Banded Crake
		Red-legged Crake
	tricolor	Red-necked Rail
		Tri-coloured Rail
Aramides	*axillaris*	Rufous-necked Wood Rail
		Rufous-crowned Rail
	cajanea	Grey-necked Wood Rail
		Cayenne Wood Rail
	mangle	Little Wood Rail
		Spix's Wood Rail
	ypecaha	Giant Wood Rail
		Ypecaha Wood Rail

FAMILY/GENUS	SPECIES/SUBSPECIES	ENGLISH NAMES
Crex	*crex*	Corncrake
		Land Rail
Porzana	*albicollis*	Ash-throated Crake
		White-throated Rail
	carolina	Sora
		Sora Rail
		Carolina Crake
	cinerea	Ashy Crake
		White-browed Crake
	fusca	Ruddy-breasted Crake
		Ruddy Crake
	paykullii	Band-bellied Crake
		Chestnut-breasted Crake
	pusilla	Baillon's Crake
		Marsh Crake
	tabuensis	Sooty Rail
		Spotted Crake
Laterallus	*exilis*	Grey-breasted Crake
		Temminck's Crake
	ruber	Ruddy Crake
		Red Rail
	spilopterus	Dot-winged Crake
		Spot-winged Crake
Coturnicops	*notata*	Speckled Crake
		Marked Rail
		Darwin's Rail

(All species of genus *Sarothrura* alternatively known as Crakes, Pygmy Rails or Flufftails.)

Sarothrura	*affinis*	Chestnut-tailed Crake
		Red-tailed Flufftail
	ayresi	White-winged Crake
		Ayres's Crake
	bohmi	Bohm's Crake
		Streaky-breasted Flufftail
	lugens	Chestnut-headed Crake
		Long-toed Flufftail
Tribonyx	*ventralis*	Black-tailed Waterhen
		Black-tailed Native Hen
Amaurornis	*isabellina*	White-breasted Waterhen
		White-breasted Swamp Hen
		White-breasted Moorhen

FAMILY/GENUS	SPECIES/SUBSPECIES	ENGLISH NAMES

Rallidae Rails, Coots, Gallinules (cont.)

Gallinula	*chloropus*	Grey Moorhen
		Moorhen
		Waterhen
		Common Gallinule
Porphyrula	*alleni*	Allen's Gallinule
		Allen's Reed Hen
		Lesser Reed Hen
	flavirostris	Azure Gallinule
		Little Gallinule
Porphyrio	*porphyrio*	Purple Swamp Hen
		Purple Gallinule*
		Blue Gallinule
		King Reed Hen
		Purple Moorhen
Fulica	*cristata*	Crested Coot
		Red-knobbed Coot

Cariamidae Seriemas

Cariama	*cristata*	Red-legged Seriema
		Crested Seriema
		Crested Cariama
	burmeisteri	Black-legged Seriema
		Burmeister's Seriema

Otididae Bustards

Neotis	*denhami*	Denham's Bustard
		Stanley's Bustard
Ardeotis	*arabs*	Great Arabian Bustard
		Sudan Bustard

(All species of genus *Eupodotis* alternatively known as Bustards or Korhaans.)

Eupodotis	*atra*	Little Black Bustard
		Black Korhaan
		White-quilled Bustard
	humilis	Somali Black-throated Bustard
		Little Brown Bustard
	melanogaster	Black-bellied Korhaan
		Long-legged Korhaan
	ruficrista	Crested Bustard
		Red-crested Korhaan

FAMILY/GENUS	SPECIES/SUBSPECIES	ENGLISH NAMES
	senegalensis	Senegal Bustard
		White-breasted Bustard
		White-bellied Korhaan
	vigorsi	Black-throated Bustard
		Karroo Korhaan
		Vaac Korhaan
Sypheotides	*indica*	Lesser Florican
		Likh Florican
		Likh

Jacanidae Jacanas

Microparra	*capensis*	Smaller Jacana
		Lesser Jacana
Irediparra	*gallinacea*	Comb-crested Jacana
		Lotus Bird

Charadriidae Plovers, Dotterels

(Many species of genus *Vanellus* alternatively known as Plovers or Lapwings.)

Vanellus	*albiceps*	White-headed Plover
		White-crowned Plover
		Black-shouldered Wattled Plover
	chilensis	Southern Lapwing
		Chilean Lapwing
	lugubris	Senegal Plover
		Lesser Black-winged Plover
	spinosus	Spur-winged Lapwing
		Masked Lapwing
	vanellus	Lapwing
		Northern Lapwing
		Green Plover
		Peewit
Pluvialis	*dominica*	American Golden Plover
		Asiatic Golden Plover
		Pacific Golden Plover
		Lesser Golden Plover
	squatarola	Black-bellied Plover
		Grey Plover

Charadriidae Plovers, Dotterels (cont.)
(Some species of genus *Charadrius* alternatively known as Plovers or Dotterels.)

Charadrius	*alexandrinus*	Snow Plover
		Kentish Plover
	bicinctus	Banded Dotterel
		Double-banded Dotterel
	forbesi	Forbes's Banded Plover
		Forbes's Plover
	leschenaultii	Greater Sand Plover
		Large Sand Plover
		Geoffroy's Sand Plover
	mongolus	Mongolian Plover
		Lesser Sand Plover
	obscurus	Red-breasted Dotterel
		New Zealand Dotterel
	pecuarius	Kittlitz's Plover
		Kittlitz's Sand Plover

Scolopacidae	Snipe, Sandpipers	
Bartramia	*longicauda*	Upland Sandpiper
		Upland Plover
		Bartram's Sandpiper
Numenius	*madagascariensis*	Far Eastern Curlew
		Eastern Curlew
		Long-billed Curlew
	minutus	Little Curlew
		Little Whimbrel
Tringa	*brevipes*	Grey-tailed Tattler
		Grey-rumped Sandpiper
		Siberian Tattler
	guttifer	Spotted Greenshank
		Nordmann's Greenshank
		Armstrong's Sandpiper
Gallinago	*imperialis*	Banded Snipe
		Imperial Snipe
Arenaria	*interpres*	Ruddy Turnstone
		Turnstone
Limnodromus	*griseus*	Short-billed Dowitcher
		Red-breasted Snipe
Coenocorypha	*aucklandica*	Sub-antarctic Snipe

		Auckland Snipe
Calidris	*acuminata*	Sharp-tailed Sandpiper
		Siberian Pectoral Sandpiper
	canutus	Red Knot
		Knot
		Eastern Knot★
	fuscicollis	White-rumped Sandpiper
		Bonaparte's Sandpiper
	ruficollis	Rufous-necked Sandpiper
		Red-necked Stint
	tenuirostris	Great Knot
		Eastern Knot★

Recurvirostridae   Avocets, Stilts

Cladorhynchus	*leucocephalus*	Banded Stilt
		Pied Stilt
Recurvirostra	*avosetta*	Avocet
		Black-crowned Avocet

Phalaropodidae   Phalaropes

Phalaropus	*fulicarius*	Red Phalarope
		Grey Phalarope
	lobatus	Northern Phalarope
		Red-necked Phalarope

Burhinidae   Thick-knees

(All species alternatively known as Stone Curlews or Thick-knees.)

Burhinus	*bistriatus*	Double-striped Thick-knee
		Mexican Stone Curlew
	capensis	Spotted Thick-knee
		Spotted Dikkop
	magnirostris	Southern Stone Curlew
		Bush Curlew
	oedicnemus	Stone Curlew
		Norfolk Plover
	vermiculatus	Water Thick-knee
		Water Dikkop
Esacus	*recurvirostris*	Great Stone Curlew
		Oriental Thick-knee

Glareolidae   Coursers, Pratincoles

Pluvianus	*aegyptius*	Egyptian Plover
		Crocodile Bird
Cursorius	*chalcopterus*	Violet-tipped Courser
		Bronze-winged Courser
	cinctus	Heuglin's Courser
		Three-banded Courser
Glareola	*maldivarum*	Eastern Collared Pratincole
		Oriental Collared Pratincole
		Oriental Pratincole
	nuchalis	White-collared Pratincole
		Rock Pratincole
	pratincola	Collared Pratincole
		Common Pratincole

Thinocoridae   Seedsnipe

Thinocorus	*rumicivorus*	Least Seedsnipe
		Patagonian Seedsnipe

Stercorariidae   Skuas, Jaegers

Stercorarius	*longicaudus*	Long-tailed Jaeger
		Long-tailed Skua
		Buffon's Skua
	maccormicki	MacCormick's Skua
		Antarctic Skua
	parasiticus	Parasitic Jaeger
		Arctic Skua
		Richardson's Skua
	skua	Great Skua
		Bonxie

Laridae   Gulls, Terns

Larus	*belcheri*	Band-tailed Gull
		Simeon Gull
		Belcher's Gull
	bulleri	Black-billed Gull
		Buller's Gull
	canus	Common Gull
		Mew Gull
	crassirostris	Black-tailed Gull
		Japanese Gull

FAMILY/GENUS	SPECIES/SUBSPECIES	ENGLISH NAMES
	dominicanus	Kelp Gull
		Southern Black-backed Gull
	fulginosus	Lava Gull
		Dusky Gull
	hemprichii	Sooty Gull
		Aden Gull
		Hemprich's Gull
	relictus	Relict Gull
		Mongolian Gull
	scoresbii	Dolphin Gull
		Magellan Gull
Sterna	*albifrons*	Least Tern
		Little Tern
	bergii	Greater Crested Tern
		Swift Tern
	hirundinacea	South American Tern
		Cassin's Tern
	lunata	Grey-backed Tern
		Spectacled Tern
	nereis	Fairy Tern*
		Nere's Tern
	saundersi	Saunder's Little Tern
		Black-shafted Tern
	superciliaris	Yellow-billed Tern
		Amazon Tern
	vittata	Antarctic Tern
		Wreathed Tern
Procelsterna	*caerulea*	Blue-grey Noddy
		Grey Ternlet
Anous	*stolidus*	Brown Noddy
		Common Noddy
Gygis	*alba*	White Tern
		Fairy Tern*

Alcidae Auks, Murres

Alle	*alle*	Dovekie
		Little Auk
		Rotch
Uria	*aalge*	Common Murre
		Guillemot
		Thin-billed Murre

Alcidae Auks, Murres (cont.)

	lomvia	Thick-billed Murre
		Arctic Guillemot
		Brünnich's Guillemot
		Brünnich's Murre
Cepphus	*grylle*	Black Guillemot
		Tystie

Pteroclidae   Sandgrouse

Pterocles	*burchelli*	Variegated Sandgrouse
		Burchell's Sandgrouse
		Spotted Sandgrouse
	coronatus	Coronated Sandgrouse
		Crowned Sandgrouse
	exustus	Chestnut-bellied Sandgrouse
		Chestnut-breasted Sandgrouse
	personatus	Madagascar Sandgrouse
		Masked Sandgrouse
		Gould's Sandgrouse

Columbidae   Pigeons, Doves

(Many species alternatively known as Pigeons or Doves. Ground Doves, Fruit Doves and Turtle Doves often referred to simply as Doves. The names Collared Dove and Turtle Dove are often transposed. Where these are the only differences the names are not included.)

Columba	*argentina*	Grey Wood Pigeon*
		Silver Pigeon
	arquatrix	Olive Pigeon
		Rameron Pigeon
		Yellow-eyed Pigeon
	caribaea	Ring-tailed Pigeon
		Jamaican Pigeon
		Jamaican Band-tailed Pigeon
	cayennensis	Pale-vented Pigeon
		Rufous Pigeon
	goodsoni	Dusky Pigeon
		Goodson's Pigeon
	guinea	Speckled Pigeon
		Guinea Pigeon
		Triangular-spotted Pigeon
		Cape Rock Pigeon

FAMILY/GENUS	SPECIES/SUBSPECIES	ENGLISH NAMES
	hodgsonii	Speckled Wood Pigeon
		Hodgson's Wood Pigeon
		Jungle Pigeon
	janthina	Japanese Wood Pigeon
		Black Pigeon
	junoniae	Laurel Pigeon
		Canarian Pigeon
	livia	Rock Dove
		Blue Rock Pigeon
	maculosa	Spot-winged Pigeon
		Spotted Pigeon
	mayeri	Mauritius Pink Pigeon
		Mayer's Pigeon
	oenops	Peruvian Pigeon
		Salvin's Pigeon
	palumbus	Wood Pigeon
		Ring Dove
	punicea	Purple Wood Pigeon
		Pale-capped Pigeon
	rupestris	Blue Hill Pigeon
		Eastern Rock Pigeon
	speciosa	Scaled Pigeon
		Fair Pigeon
		Splendid Pigeon
	squamosa	Scaly-naped Pigeon
		Red-necked Pigeon
		West Indian Pigeon
	trocaz	Long-toed Pigeon
		Madeiran Pigeon
	unicincta	Scaly Grey Pigeon
		African Wood Pigeon
		Congo Wood Pigeon
		Grey Wood Pigeon★
	vitiensis	Metallic Wood Pigeon
		White-throated Pigeon
Streptopelia	*bitorquata*	Javanese Turtle Dove
		Double-collared Turtle Dove
	capicola	Ring-necked Dove
		Cape Ring Dove
		Cape Turtle Dove
	chinensis	Spotted Dove

Columbidae Pigeons, Doves (cont.)

	Necklace Dove
	Chinese Necklace Dove
	Chinese Spotted Turtle Dove
	Chinese Spotted Dove
	Pearl-necked Dove
decaocto	Collared Turtle Dove
	Collared Dove
	Indian Ring-necked Dove
decipiens	African Mourning Dove
	Deceptive Ring Dove
	Angola Dove
lugens	Pink-breasted Dove
	African Turtle Dove
	Pink-breasted Turtle Dove
	Dusky Dove
	Black Dove
orientalis	Rufous Turtle Dove
	Oriental Turtle Dove
picturata	Madagascar Turtle Dove
	Painted Dove
reichenowi	White-winged Collared Dove
	Reichenow's Dove
risoria	Ringed Turtle Dove
	Barbary Dove
	Blond Ring Dove
	Domestic Ringed Dove
	Domestic Collared Dove
roseogrisea	Pink-headed Turtle Dove
	African Collared Dove
	African Ring Dove
	Rose-grey Dove
semitorquata	Red-eyed Dove
	Half-collared Ring Dove
senegalensis	Laughing Dove
	Palm Dove
	Palm Turtle Dove
	Little Brown Dove
	Senegal Dove
tranquebarica	Red Turtle Dove
	Dwarf Turtle Dove

FAMILY/GENUS	SPECIES/SUBSPECIES	ENGLISH NAMES
Geopelia	*cuneata*	Diamond Dove
		Little Turtle Dove
	striata	Barred Ground Dove
		Peaceful Dove
		Zebra Dove
		Four O'Clock Dove
Aplopelia	*larvata*	Lemon Dove
		Rufous-necked Wood Dove
Macropygia	*amboinensis*	Amboina Cuckoo Dove
		Pink-breasted Cuckoo Dove
	phasianella	Red Cuckoo Dove
		Large Brown Cuckoo Dove
		Brown Cuckoo Dove
		Brown Pigeon
		Pheasant-tailed Cuckoo Dove
	ruficeps	Lesser Red Cuckoo Dove
		Red-headed Cuckoo Dove
		Little Cuckoo Dove
	unchall	Barred Cuckoo Dove
		Bar-tailed Cuckoo Dove
Oena	*capensis*	Namaqua Dove
		Cape Dove
		Masked Dove
		Long-tailed Dove
		Harlequin Dove
Turtur	*abyssinicus*	Black-billed Blue-spotted Wood Dove
		Black-billed Wood Dove
	afer	Blue-spotted Wood Dove
		Sapphire-spotted Dove
		Red-billed Wood Dove
	chalcospilos	Emerald-spotted Wood Dove
		Green-spotted Wood Dove
	tympanistria	Tambourine Dove
		White-breasted Wood Dove
		Forest Dove
Chalcophaps	*indica*	Emerald Dove
		Indian Green-winged Dove
		Green-winged Dove
		Green-backed Dove
	stephani	Brown-backed Ground Pigeon
		Brown-backed Emerald Dove

FAMILY/GENUS	SPECIES/SUBSPECIES	ENGLISH NAMES

Columbidae Pigeons, Doves (cont.)

		Stephani's Green-winged Dove
Henicophaps	*albifrons*	White-capped Ground Pigeon
		White-fronted Pigeon
		Black Bronzewing
	foersteri	New Britain Ground Pigeon
		New Britain Bronzewing
Petrophassa	*plumifera*	Plumed Pigeon
		White-bellied Plumed Pigeon
	scripta	Squatter Pigeon
		Partridge Pigeon
		Partridge Bronze-winged Pigeon
		Bare-eyed Partridge Bronze-winged Pigeon*
		Blue-eyed Partridge Bronzewing
	smithii	Partridge Pigeon
		Smith's Partridge Pigeon
		Bare-eyed Partridge Bronzewing*
Phaps	*chalcoptera*	Common Bronzewing
		Bronze-winged Pigeon
	elegans	Brush Bronzewing
		Brush Bronze-winged Pigeon
	histrionica	Flock Pigeon
		Harlequin Pigeon
Ocyphaps	*lophotes*	Crested Pigeon
		Crested Bronze-winged Pigeon
		Australian Crested Pigeon
Zenaida	*auriculata*	Eared Dove
		Blue-eared Dove
	macroura	Mourning Dove
		Carolina Dove
Columbina	*cruziana*	Croaking Ground Dove
		Gold-billed Ground Dove
		Peruvian Ground Dove
		Yellow-billed Ground Dove
	minuta	Plain-breasted Ground Dove
		Grey Ground Dove
		Pigmy Dove
	passerina	Common Ground Dove
		Scaly-breasted Ground Dove
		Rosy Dove

		Passerine Ground Dove
	squamata	Scaled Dove
		Scaly Dove
	talpacoti	Ruddy Ground Dove
		Cinnamon Dove
		Stone Dove
		Talpacoti Dove
Claravis	*godefrida*	Purple-winged Ground Dove
		Purple-barred Ground Dove
		Geoffrey's Ground Dove
	mondetoura	Maroon-chested Ground Dove
		Purple-breasted Ground Dove
	pretiosa	Blue Ground Dove
		Cinerous Ground Dove
Metriopelia	*aymara*	Golden-spotted Ground Dove
		Bronze-winged Ground Dove
	ceciliae	Bare-faced Ground Dove
		Spectacled Dove
Leptotila	*cassinii*	Grey-chested Dove
		Cassin's Ground Dove
		Cassin Dove
	jamaicensis	White-bellied Dove
		Jamaican Ground Dove
		Caribbean Dove
		Violet Dove
		Amethyst Dove
	megalura	Large-tailed Dove
		White-faced Dove
	ochraceiventris	Ochre-bellied Dove
		Buff-bellied Dove
	verreauxi	White-fronted Dove
		White-tipped Dove
		Verreaux's Ground Dove
	wellsi	Grenada Dove
		Well's Dove
Geotrygon	*caniceps*	Grey-headed Quail Dove
		Grey-faced Quail Dove
	chrysia	Key West Quail Dove
		Golden Dove
	frenata	White-throated Quail Dove
		Pink-faced Quail Dove

Columbidae Pigeons, Doves (cont.)

	linearis	Lined Quail Dove
		White-faced Dove
		Venezuelan Quail Dove
	mystacea	Bridled Quail Dove
		Moustache Quail Dove
	versicolor	Crested Quail Dove
		Mountain Witch Dove
Gallicolumba	*beccarii*	Grey-throated Ground Dove
		Grey-breasted Quail Dove
		Beccari's Ground Pigeon
	erythroptera	Ground Dove
		Society Dove
	jobiensis	White-breasted Ground Dove
		Jobi Ground Dove
	luzonica	Luzon Bleeding-heart Pigeon
		Bleeding-heart Pigeon
		Blood-breasted Pigeon
	rubescens	Marquesas Ground Dove
		Grey-hooded Ground Dove
	rufigula	Red-throated Ground Dove
		Golden-heart Pigeon
	stairii	Friendly Ground Dove
		Stair's Ground Dove
	tristigmata	Celebes Quail Dove
		Celebes Ground Dove
	xanthonura	White-throated Ground Dove
		Buff-hooded Ground Dove

(All species of genus *Goura* alternatively known as Crowned Pigeons or Gouras.)

Goura	*cristata*	Common Crowned Pigeon
		Blue Crowned Pigeon
	scheepmakeri	Sheepmaker's Crowned Pigeon
		Maroon-breasted Crowned Pigeon
		Sclater's Crowned Pigeon
Phapitreron	*amethystina*	Greater Brown Fruit Dove
		Amethyst Brown Fruit Dove
	leucotis	Lesser Brown Fruit Dove
		White-eared Brown Fruit Dove

(All species of genus *Treron* alternatively known as Pigeons or Green Pigeons.)

Treron	*australis*	African Green Pigeon
		Green Fruit Pigeon
		Madagascar Green Pigeon
	formosae	Whistling Green Pigeon
		Formosan Green Pigeon
	seimundi	White-bellied Pintail Green Pigeon
		Yellow-vented Pigeon
	sieboldii	Green Pigeon
		White-bellied Pigeon
		White-bellied Wedge-tailed Pigeon
		Japanese Green Pigeon
		Siebold's Pigeon
	waalia	Bruce's Green Pigeon
		Waalia Fruit Pigeon
		Yellow-bellied Pigeon
Ptilinopus	*bellus*	Purple-bellied Fruit Pigeon
		Charming Fruit Pigeon
	cinctus	Black-backed Fruit Dove
		Yellow-bellied Fruit Dove
	coronulatus	Little Coronated Fruit Dove
		Lilac-capped Fruit Pigeon
	dohertyi	Red-naped Fruit Dove
		Doherty's Fruit Dove
	greyii	Red-bellied Fruit Dove
		Grey's Fruit Dove
	layardi	Velvet Dove
		Yellow-headed Dove
	leclancheri	Black-chinned Fruit Dove
		Leclancher's Dove
	luteovirens	Golden Dove
		Lemon Dove
	melanospila	Black-naped Fruit Dove
		Blue-naped Fruit Dove
	naina	Small Green Fruit Dove
		Dwarf Fruit Dove
	perlatus	Pink-spotted Fruit Dove
		Spotted Fruit Dove
	perousii	Many-coloured Fruit Dove
		Rainbow Fruit Dove

Columbidae Pigeons, Doves (cont.)

	porphyraceus	Crimson-crowned Fruit Dove
		Ponape Fruit Dove
	pulchellus	Beautiful Fruit Dove
		Pretty Fruit Dove
		Crimson-capped Fruit Dove
	regina	Swainson's Fruit Dove
		Pink-capped Dove
	rivoli	White-breasted Fruit Dove
		Rivoli's Fruit Dove
		White-bibbed Dove
		Moon Dove
	roseicapillus	Marianas Fruit Dove
		Pink-crowned Fruit Dove
		Rose-crowned Fruit Dove
	solomonensis	Splendid Fruit Dove
		Yellow-bibbed Fruit Dove
		Solomon Fruit Dove
	subgularis	Dark-chinned Fruit Dove
		Chestnut-chinned Fruit Dove
	tannensis	Tanna Fruit Dove
		Silver-shouldered Fruit Dove
	viridis	Red-breasted Fruit Dove
		Red-bibbed Dove
Alectroenas	*madagascariensis*	Madagascar Blue Pigeon
		Madagascar Blue Wart Pigeon
		Madagascar Wart Pigeon
	pulcherrima	Seychelles Blue Pigeon
		Red-crowned Blue Wart Pigeon
		Red-crowned Wart Pigeon
	sganzini	Comoro Blue Pigeon
		Sganzin's Blue Wart Pigeon
		Sganzin's Wart Pigeon
Ducula	*aenea*	Green Imperial Pigeon
		Imperial Fruit Pigeon★
	badia	Imperial Pigeon
		Mountain Imperial Pigeon
	basilica	Moluccan Rufous-bellied Pigeon
		Basilica Pigeon
	bicolor	Pied Imperial Pigeon
		White Imperial Pigeon

FAMILY/GENUS	SPECIES/SUBSPECIES	ENGLISH NAMES
		White Fruit Pigeon
	chalconota	Red-breasted Imperial Pigeon
		Shining Fruit Pigeon
	cineracea	Timor Imperial Pigeon
		Ashy Imperial Pigeon
	concinna	Elegant Imperial Pigeon
		Imperial Fruit Pigeon★
		Gold-eyed Pigeon
	goliath	Giant Pigeon
		Goliath Imperial Pigeon
	lacernulata	Black-backed Imperial Pigeon
		Dark-backed Imperial Pigeon
	latrans	Peale's Pigeon
		Fiji Imperial Pigeon
	melanochroa	Black Imperial Pigeon★
		Silver-laced Pigeon
	mindorensis	Mindora Imperial Pigeon
		Zone-tailed Pigeon
	myristicivora	Island Imperial Pigeon★
		New Guinea Imperial Pigeon
		Black-knobbed Imperial Pigeon
	oceanica	Micronesian Pigeon
		Oceanic Fruit Pigeon
	perspicillata	White-eyed Imperial Pigeon
		Spectacled Imperial Pigeon
	pistrinaria	Grey Imperial Pigeon
		Island Imperial Pigeon★
	poliocephala	Pink-bellied Imperial Pigeon
		Grey-faced Pigeon
		Grey-faced Zone-tailed Pigeon
	rufigaster	Purple-tailed Imperial Pigeon
		Red-breasted Imperial Pigeon
		Rufous-bellied Imperial Pigeon
	spilorrhoa	Torres Strait Imperial Pigeon
		Nutmeg Pigeon
	whartoni	Christmas Island Imperial Pigeon
		Black Imperial Pigeon★
	zoeae	Banded Imperial Pigeon
		Zoe's Imperial Pigeon
Gymnophaps	*albertisii*	Bare-eyed Mountain Pigeon
		D'Albertis's Mountain Pigeon

Loriidae   Lories, Lorikeets
(Many species known alternatively as Lories or Lorikeets.)

Chalcopsitta	*atra insignia*	Rajah Lory
		Raja Lory
		Red-quilled Lory
	duivenbodei	Duyvenbode's Lory
		Brown Lory
	scintillata	Yellow-streaked Lory
		Cream-streaked Lory
		Red-fronted Lory
Eos	*cyanogenia*	Black-winged Lory
		Blue-cheeked Lory
	histrio	Red and Blue Lory
		Blue-tailed Lory
		Blue-diademed Lory
	reticulata	Blue-streaked Lory
		Blue-necked Lory
	semilarvata	Blue-eared Lory
		Half-masked Lory
		Ceram Lory
	squamata	Violet-necked Lory
		Violet-headed Lory
		Violet-naped Lory
		Wallace's Violet-necked Lory
		Moluccas Red Lory
Pseudeos	*fuscata*	Dusky Lory
		White-backed Lory
		White-rumped Lory
Trichoglossus	*chlorolepidotus*	Scaly-breasted Lorikeet
		Green Lorikeet
		Gold and Green Lorikeet
	euteles	Perfect Lorikeet
		Yellow-headed Lorikeet
	flavoviridis	Yellow and Green Lorikeet
		Yellow-Green Lorikeet
		Sula Lorikeet
	haematodus	
	haematodus	Rainbow Lory
		Green-naped Lorikeet
	h. capistratus	Edward's Lorikeet
		Blue-faced Lorikeet

FAMILY/GENUS	SPECIES/SUBSPECIES	ENGLISH NAMES
	h. massena	Coconut Lory
		Massena's Lorikeet
	h. moluccanus	Rainbow Lorikeet
		Swainson's Lorikeet
		Blue Mountain Lorikeet
	johnstoniae	Johnstone's Lorikeet
		Mrs Johnstone's Lorikeet
		Mount Apo Lorikeet
	ornatus	Ornate Lory
		Ornamented Lorikeet
	rubiginosus	Ponape Lory
		Cherry-red Lorikeet
		Caroline Lorikeet
	versicolor	Varied Lorikeet
		Variegated Lorikeet
		Red-crowned Lorikeet
Lorius	*amabilis*	Stresemann's Lory
		New Britain Lory
	chlorocercus	Yellow-bibbed Lory
		Green-tailed Lory
		Gould's Lory
	domicellus	Purple-naped Lory
		Purple-capped Lory
	garrulus	Chattering Lory
		Scarlet Lory
	hypoinochrous	Purple-bellied Lory
		Louisiade Lory
	lory	Black-capped Lory
		Tri-coloured Lory
Phigys	*solitarius*	Collared Lory
		Solitary Lory
		Ruffed Lory
		Fiji Lory
Vini	*australis*	Blue-crowned Lory
		Blue-crested Lory
		Samoan Lory
	kuhlii	Kuhl's Lory
		Kuhl's Ruffed Lory
		Ruby Lory
	peruviana	Tahitian Lory
		Tahiti Blue Lory

Loriidae Lories, Lorikeets (cont.)

		White-throated Lory
	stepheni	Stephen's Lory
		Henderson Island Lory
	ultramarina	Ultramarine Lory
		Goupil's Lory
		Marquesas Lory
Charmosyna	*diadema*	New Caledonian Lorikeet
		New Caledonia Diademed Lorikeet
		Diademed Lorikeet
	margarethae	Duchess Lorikeet
		Princess Margaret's Lorikeet
	multistriata	Striated Lorikeet
		Many-striped Lorikeet
		Yellow-streaked Lory
	placentis	Red-flanked Lorikeet
		Pleasing Lorikeet
		Beautiful Lorikeet
	pulchella	Fairy Lorikeet
		Fair Lorikeet
	rubrigularis	Red-chinned Lorikeet
		Red-throated Lorikeet*
	rubronotata	Red-spotted Lorikeet
		Red-rumped Lorikeet
		Red-marked Lorikeet
	toxopei	Blue-fronted Lorikeet
		Buru Lorikeet
		Toxopeus's Lorikeet
Oreopsittacus	*arfaki*	Whiskered Lorikeet
		Blue-cheeked Lorikeet
		Blue-cheeked Alpine Lorikeet
		Arfak Alpine Lorikeet
		Arfak Lorikeet
		Alpine Lory
Neopsittacus	*pullicauda*	Emerald Lorikeet
		Alpine Lorikeet
		Mountain Lory

Cacatuidae Cockatoos

Probosciger	*aterrimus*	Palm Cockatoo
		Great Palm Cockatoo

FAMILY/GENUS	SPECIES/SUBSPECIES	ENGLISH NAMES
		Great Black Cockatoo
		Cape York Cockatoo
		Black Macaw
Calyptorhynchus	*funereus funereus*	Yellow-tailed Cockatoo
		Yellow-tailed Black Cockatoo
		Funereal Cockatoo
	f. baudinii	White-tailed Cockatoo
		White-tailed Black Cockatoo
		Baudin's Cockatoo
		Baudin's Black Cockatoo
	lathami	Glossy Cockatoo
		Glossy Black Cockatoo
		Latham's Cockatoo
		Leach's Cockatoo
	magnificus	Red-tailed Cockatoo
		Red-tailed Black Cockatoo
		Banksian Cockatoo
		Banks's Black Cockatoo
Callocephalon	*fimbriatum*	Gang Gang Cockatoo
		Red-crowned Cockatoo
		Helmeted Cockatoo
Eolophus	*roseicapillus*	Galah
		Roseate Cockatoo
		Rose-breasted Cockatoo
		Red-breasted Cockatoo
Cacatua	*alba*	White Cockatoo
		Great White Cockatoo
		White-crested Cockatoo
		Umbrella Cockatoo
	ducorpsii	Ducorps's Cockatoo
		Solomon Islands Cockatoo
	galerita	Sulphur-crested Cockatoo
		Greater Sulphur-crested Cockatoo
		White Cockatoo
	haematuropygia	Red-vented Cockatoo
		Philippine Cockatoo
	leadbeateri	Leadbeater's Cockatoo
		Major Mitchell's Cockatoo
		Pink Cockatoo
	moluccensis	Salmon-crested Cockatoo
		Pink-crested Cockatoo

FAMILY/GENUS	SPECIES/SUBSPECIES	ENGLISH NAMES

Cacatuidae Cockatoos (cont.)

		Rose-crested Cockatoo
		Moluccan Cockatoo
	sanguinea	Little Corella
		Bare-eyed Cockatoo
		Blue-eyed Cockatoo★
		Blood-stained Cockatoo
		Short-billed Cockatoo
	sulphurea parvula	Dwarf Sulphur-crested Cockatoo
		Timor Cockatoo
	tenuirostris	Long-billed Corella
		Slender-billed Corella
		Long-billed Cockatoo
Nymphicus	*hollandicus*	Cockatiel
		Quarrion

Psittacidae Parrots, Lovebirds, Macaws

Nestor	*notabilis*	Kea
		Mountain Parrot
Micropsitta	*bruijnii*	Red-breasted Pygmy Parrot
		Mountain Pygmy Parrot
		Bruijn's Pygmy Parrot
		Bruijn's Red-headed Pygmy Parrot
	keiensis	Yellow-capped Pygmy Parrot
		Kei Islands Pygmy Parrot
	pusio	Buff-faced Pygmy Parrot
		Blue-crowned Pygmy Parrot
		Little Pygmy Parrot
Opopsitta	*diophthalma*	
	diophthalma	Double-eyed Fig Parrot
		Double-eyed Dwarf Parrot
		Dwarf Fig Parrot
		Lorilet
	d. coxeni	Coxen's Fig Parrot
		Coxen's Double-eyed Fig Parrot
		Coxen's Two-eyed Fig Parrot
		Coxen's Blue-browed Fig Parrot
		Blue-browed Fig Parrot
		Blue-browed Lorilet
		Red-faced Lorilet
		Coxen's Lorilet
	d. macleayana	Red-browed Fig Parrot

FAMILY/GENUS	SPECIES/SUBSPECIES	ENGLISH NAMES
		Blue-faced Fig Parrot
		Macleay's Lorilet
	gulielmiterti	Orange-breasted Fig Parrot
		King of Holland's Fig Parrot
Psittaculirostris	*desmarestii*	Desmarest's Fig Parrot
		Desmarest's Dwarf Parrot
		Golden-headed Fig Parrot
		Golden-headed Dwarf Parrot

(All species of genus *Psittacella* sometimes known as Tiger Parrots.)

Psittacella	*brehmii*	Brehm's Parrot
		Brehm's Ground Parrot
	madaraszi	Madarasz's Parrot
		Madarasz's Ground Parrot
		Plain-breasted Little Parrot
	modesta	Modest Parrot
		Modest Ground Parrot
		Barred Little Parrot
	picta	Painted Parrot
		Painted Ground Parrot
		Mount Victoria Ground Parrot
		Timberline Parrot
Geoffroyus	*geoffroyi*	Red-cheeked Parrot
		Red-cheeked Geoffroy's Parrot
		Geoffroy's Parrot
		Geoffroy's Song Parrot
	heteroclitus	Singing Parrot
		Yellow-headed Song Parrot
		Yellow-headed Geoffroy's Parrot
		New Britain Yellow-headed Parrot
		New Ireland Yellow-headed Parrot
	simplex	Blue-collared Parrot
		Lilac-collared Song Parrot
		Lilac-collared Geoffroy's Parrot
Prioniturus	*discurus*	Blue-crowned Racket-tailed Parrot
		Philippine Racket-tailed Parrot
	flavicans	Red-spotted Racket-tailed Parrot
		Crimson-spotted Racket-tailed Parrot
		Red-crowned Racket-tailed Parrot
	luconensis	Green Racket-tailed Parrot
		Luzon Racket-tailed Parrot
		Green-headed Racket-tailed Parrot

Psittacidae Parrots, Lovebirds, Macaws (cont.)

	mada	Buru Racket-tailed Parrot
		Mount Mada Racket-tailed Parrot
	montanus	Mountain Racket-tailed Parrot
		Luzon Crimson-spotted Racket-tailed Parrot
	platurus	Golden-mantled Racket-tailed Parrot
		Racket-tailed Parrot
		Celebes Racket-tailed Parrot

(All species of genus *Tanygnathus* sometimes known as Great-billed Parrots.)

Tanygnathus	*gramineus*	Black-lored Parrot
		Buru Green Parrot
	heterurus	Rufous-tailed Parrot
		Salvadori's Green Parrot
	lucionensis	Blue-naped Parrot
		Blue-crowned Green Parrot
		Philippine Green Parrot
		Luzon Parrot
	megalorynchos	Great-billed Parrot
		Large-billed Parrot
		Island Parrot
		Moluccan Parrot
	sumatranus	Muller's Parrot
		Muller's Blue-backed Parrot
		Blue-backed Parrot
Eclectus	*roratus roratus*	Grand Eclectus Parrot
		King Parrot★
		Temple Parrot
	r. polychloros	Red-sided Eclectus Parrot
		Red-sided Parrot
Prosopeia	*personata*	Masked Shining Parrot
		Masked Musk Parakeet
		Masked Parakeet
		Yellow-breasted Musk Parakeet
	tabuensis	Red-breasted Musk Parakeet
		Maroon Musk Parakeet
		Maroon Parakeet
		Red Shining Parrot
		Tabuan Parakeet
Alisterus	*amboinensis*	Amboina King Parrot
		Island King Parrot

FAMILY/GENUS	SPECIES/SUBSPECIES	ENGLISH NAMES
		Amboina Red Parakeet
	chloropterus	Green-winged King Parrot
		Papuan King Parrot
	scapularis	Australian King Parrot
		King Parrot★
		Scarlet and Green Parrot
Aprosmictus	*erythropterus*	Red-winged Parrot
		Red-shouldered Parrot
		Blood-winged Parrot
		Crimson-winged Parrot
	jonquillaceus	Timor Red-winged Parrot
		Timor Crimson-winged Parrot
Polytelis	*alexandrae*	Princess Parrot
		Princess of Wales Parakeet
		Princess Alexandra's Parakeet
		Queen Alexandra's Parakeet
		Alexandra Parakeet
		Alexandrine Parakeet★
		Rose-throated Parakeet
		Spinifex Parrot
	anthopeplus	Regent Parrot
		Rock Peplar Parakeet
		Rock Pebbler Parakeet
		Black-tailed Parakeet
		Mountain Parakeet
	swainsonii	Superb Parrot
		Barraband Parrot
		Barraband's Parrot
Purpurei-cephalus	*spurius*	Red-capped Parrot★
		Pileated Parakeet
		Australian Red-capped Parakeet
		King Parrot★
Barnardius	*barnardi*	Mallee Ringneck Parrot
		Mallee Parakeet
		Ring-necked Parakeet
		Barnard's Parakeet
		Buln Buln
	zonarius zonarius	Port Lincoln Parrot
		Yellow-collared Parrot
		Zoned Parrot
		Bauer's Parakeet

Psittacidae Parrots, Lovebirds, Macaws (cont.)

	z. semitorquatus	Twenty-eight Parrot
		Yellow-collared Parakeet
		Yellow-naped Parakeet
Platycercus	*adscitus*	Pale-headed Rosella
		Mealy Rosella
		Blue Rosella
	caledonicus	Green Rosella
		Tasmanian Rosella
		Yellow-bellied Rosella
		Yellow-breasted Parakeet
	elegans	Crimson Rosella
		Pennant's Parakeet
		Mountain Lowry
		Mountain Parrot
	eximius eximius	Eastern Rosella
		Common Rosella
		Rosella
		Red Rosella
		Rosella Parakeet
		Nonpareil Parrot
	e. cecilae	Golden-mantled Rosella
		Yellow-mantled Rosella
		Splendid Rosella
	flaveolus	Yellow Rosella
		Yellow-rumped Rosella
		Yellow-breasted Parakeet
	icterotis	Western Rosella
		Stanley Parakeet
		Yellow-cheeked Rosella
	venustus	Northern Rosella
		Brown's Parakeet
		Brown's Rosella
		Smutty Parrot
Psephotus	*chrysopterygius*	Golden-shouldered Parrot
		Golden-winged Parrot
		Chestnut-crowned Parrot
	haematogaster	
	narethae	Little Blue Bonnet
		Naretha Parakeet
	haematonotus	Red-rumped Parrot

FAMILY/GENUS	SPECIES/SUBSPECIES	ENGLISH NAMES
		Redrump
		Red-backed Parrot
		Scarlet-rumped Parrot
	pulcherrimus	Paradise Parrot
		Beautiful Parrot
	varius	Mulga Parrot
		Varied Parakeet
		Many-coloured Parakeet
Cyanoramphus	*auriceps*	Yellow-fronted Parakeet
		Yellow-fronted New Zealand Parakeet
		Yellow-fronted Kakariki
	malherbi	Orange-fronted Parakeet
		Alpine Parakeet
	novaezelandiae	Red-fronted Parakeet
		Red-fronted New Zealand Parakeet
		Red-fronted Kakariki
		Red-crowned Parrot*
	unicolor	Antipodes Green Parakeet
		Antipodes Island Parakeet
		Antipodes Unicolor Parakeet
		Uniform Parakeet
Eunymphicus	*cornutus*	Horned Parakeet
		Crested Parakeet

(All species of genus *Neophema* alternatively known as Parakeets or Grass Parakeets.)

Neophema	*bourkii*	Bourke's Parrot
		Bourke's Parakeet
		Blue-vented Parakeet
		Pink-bellied Parakeet
	chrysostoma	Blue-winged Parrot
		Blue-banded Parakeet
	splendida	Scarlet-chested Parrot
		Scarlet-chested Parakeet
		Splendid Parakeet
Melopsittacus	*undulatus*	Budgerigar
		Undulated Grass Parakeet [1]
		Warbling Grass Parakeet [1]
		Zebra Grass Parakeet [1]
		Scallop Parrot [1]
		Shell Parrot [1]
		Canary Parrot [1]

---

[1] These names are no longer used.

67

FAMILY/GENUS	SPECIES/SUBSPECIES	ENGLISH NAMES

Psittacidae Parrots, Lovebirds, Macaws (cont.)

FAMILY/GENUS	SPECIES/SUBSPECIES	ENGLISH NAMES
Pezoporus	*wallicus*	Ground Parrot
		Swamp Parrot
Coracopsis	*nigra*	Black Parrot
		Lesser Vasa Parrot
	vasa	Vasa Parrot
		Greater Vasa Parrot
Poicephalus	*cryptoxanthus*	Brown-headed Parrot
		Concealed-yellow Parrot
	flavifrons	Yellow-faced Parrot
		Yellow-fronted Parrot
		Shoa Parrot
	gulielmi	Jardine's Parrot
		Red-crowned Parrot*
		Congo Red-crowned Parrot
		Red-headed Parrot
	meyeri	Meyer's Parrot
		Brown Parrot
		Sudan Brown Parrot
	robustus	Cape Parrot
		Brown-necked Parrot
		Levaillant's Parrot
	rufiventris	Red-bellied Parrot
		Red-breasted Parrot
		Orange-bellied Parrot
		Abyssinian Parrot
	senegalus senegalus	Senegal Parrot
		Yellow-bellied Senegal Parrot
		Yellow-vented Senegal Parrot
	s. mesotypus	Orange-breasted Senegal Parrot
		Orange-bellied Senegal Parrot
	s. versteri	Red-vented Senegal Parrot
		Scarlet-bellied Senegal Parrot
Agapornis	*cana*	Grey-headed Lovebird
		Lavender-headed Lovebird
		Madagascar Lovebird
	lilianae	Nyasa Lovebird
		Lilian's Lovebird
	nigrigenis	Black-cheeked Lovebird
		Black-faced Lovebird*
	personata	Masked Lovebird

68

FAMILY/GENUS	SPECIES/SUBSPECIES	ENGLISH NAMES
		Black-masked Lovebird
		Black-faced Lovebird★
		Black-headed Lovebird
		Yellow-collared Lovebird
	roseicollis	Peach-faced Lovebird
		Rosy-faced Lovebird
		Rosy-headed Lovebird
		Rose-ringed Lovebird
	swinderniana	Black-collared Lovebird
		Swinderen's Lovebird
	taranta	Black-winged Lovebird
		Abyssinian Lovebird
Loriculus	*amabilis*	Moluccan Hanging Parrot
		Wallace's Hanging Parrot★
		Halmahera Hanging Parrot
	aurantiifrons	Orange-fronted Hanging Parrot
		Golden-fronted Hanging Parrot
		Misol Hanging Parrot
		Bat Lorikeet
	beryllinus	Ceylon Hanging Parrot
		Ceylon Lorikeet
	exilis	Green Hanging Parrot★
		Lilliput Hanging Parrot
		Celebes Lilliput Hanging Parrot
		Tulabula Hanging Parrot
	flosculus	Wallace's Hanging Parrot★
		Flores Hanging Parrot
	galgulus	Blue-crowned Hanging Parrot
		Sapphire-crowned Hanging Parrot
		Malay Hanging Parrot
		Malay Loriquet
	philippensis	Philippine Hanging Parrot
		Luzon Hanging Parrot
	pusillus	Yellow-throated Hanging Parrot
		Javan Hanging Parrot
		Little Hanging Parrot [1]
	stigmatus	Celebes Hanging Parrot
		Celebes Spotted Hanging Parrot
		Red-capped Hanging Parrot

---

[1] Misleading name as this is not the smallest of the Hanging Parrots in the genus.

Psittacidae Parrots, Lovebirds, Macaws (cont.)

		Red-crowned Hanging Parrot
	vernalis	Vernal Hanging Parrot
		Green Hanging Parrot★
		Indian Lorikeet
Psittacula	*alexandri*	Moustached Parakeet
		Banded Parakeet
		Bearded Parakeet
		Red-breasted Parakeet
		Pink-breasted Parakeet
	calthorpae	Emerald-collared Parakeet
		Layard's Parakeet
		Calthorp's Parakeet
	caniceps	Blyth's Parakeet
		Blyth's Nicobar Parakeet
		Grey-headed Parakeet★
	columboides	Malabar Parakeet
		Blue-winged Parakeet
	derbiana	Derbyan Parakeet
		Lord Derby's Parakeet
		Chinese Parakeet
		Upper Yangtze Parakeet
	echo	Mauritius Parakeet
		Echo Parakeet
	eupatria eupatria	Alexandrine Parakeet★
		Alexandrine Ringneck Parakeet
		Greater Rose-ringed Parakeet
		Large Indian Parakeet
	e. magnirostris	Great-billed Alexandrine Parakeet
		Andaman Parakeet
	himalayana	Slaty-headed Parakeet
		Grey-headed Parakeet★
		Hodgson's Parakeet
	krameri [1]	Rose-ringed Parakeet [1]
		Ring-necked Parakeet
		Green Parakeet
		Long-tailed Parakeet
		Senegal Long-tailed Parakeet [2]

---

[1] There is an Indian and African subspecies.   [2] African subspecies only.

FAMILY/GENUS	SPECIES/SUBSPECIES	ENGLISH NAMES
	longicauda	Long-tailed Parakeet
		Malaccan Red-cheeked Parakeet
		Malayan Red-cheeked Parakeet
	roseata	Blossom-headed Parakeet
		Rosy-headed Parakeet
Anodorhynchus	*hyacinthinus*	Hyacinth Macaw
		Hyacinthine Macaw
Cyanopsitta	*spixii*	Spix's Macaw
		Little Blue Macaw
Ara	*ambigua*	Buffon's Macaw
		Grand Military Macaw
	ararauna	Blue and Yellow Macaw
		Blue and Gold Macaw
		Yellow-breasted Macaw
	auricollis	Yellow-collared Macaw
		Golden-collared Macaw
		Yellow-naped Macaw
		Golden-naped Macaw
		Cassin's Macaw
	caninde	Caninde Macaw
		Wagler's Macaw
		Blue-throated Macaw
	chloroptera	Green-winged Macaw
		Red and Green Macaw
		Red and Blue Macaw
	couloni	Blue-headed Macaw
		Coulon's Macaw
	macao	Scarlet Macaw
		Red and Yellow Macaw
		Red, Yellow and Blue Macaw
		Red-breasted Macaw
	militaris	Military Macaw
		Great Green Macaw
	nobilis nobilis	Red-shouldered Macaw
		Hahn's Macaw
	n. longipennis	Long-winged Macaw
		Neumann's Macaw
	rubrogenys	Red-fronted Macaw
		Red-cheeked Macaw
		Lafresnaye's Macaw
	severa	Chestnut-fronted Macaw

Psittacidae Parrots, Lovebirds, Macaws (cont.)

		Severe Macaw
		Brazilian Green Macaw
Aratinga	*acuticaudata*	Blue-crowned Conure
		Sharp-tailed Conure
	aurea	Peach-fronted Conure
		Golden-crowned Conure
		Half-moon Conure★
		Brown-chested Conure
	auricapilla	Golden-capped Conure
		Gold-capped Conure
		Golden-headed Conure
	canicularis	Orange-fronted Conure
		Petz's Conure
		Half-moon Conure★
	chloroptera	Hispaniolan Conure
		San Domingo Conure
	erythrogenys	Red-masked Conure
		Red-headed Conure
	euops	Cuban Conure
		Red-speckled Conure
	guarouba	Golden Conure
		Queen of Bavaria's Conure
	holochlora	
	rubritorquis	Red-throated Conure
		Red-collared Conure
		Cut-throat Conure
	jandaya	Jandaya Conure
		Jendaya Conure
		Jenday Conure
		Yellow-headed Conure
	leucophthalmus	White-eyed Conure
		All-green Conure [1]
		Green Conure★
	nana	Olive-throated Conure
		Jamaican Conure
		Dwarf Conure
	pertinax pertinax	Brown-throated Conure
		Brown-throated Parakeet

---

[1] Misleading name as birds are not all green.

FAMILY/GENUS	SPECIES/SUBSPECIES	ENGLISH NAMES
		Caribbean Parakeet
		St Thomas's Conure
		Curaçao Conure
	p. chrysophrys	Yellow-cheeked Conure
		Orange-cheeked Conure
	solstitialis	Sun Conure
		Yellow Conure
	wagleri	Red-fronted Conure
		Wagler's Conure
	weddellii	Dusky-headed Conure
		Dusky Conure
		Weddell's Conure
Nandayus	*nenday*	Nanday Conure
		Black-headed Conure
		Black-masked Conure
		Black-hooded Conure
Leptosittaca	*branickii*	Golden-plumed Conure
		Branicki's Conure
Cyanoliseus	*patagonus*	Patagonian Conure
		Burrowing Parrot

(Many species of genus *Pyrrhura* alternatively known as Conures or Parakeets.)

FAMILY/GENUS	SPECIES/SUBSPECIES	ENGLISH NAMES
Pyrrhura	*albipectus*	White-necked Conure
		White-throated Conure
	calliptera	Brown-breasted Conure
		Flame-winged Conure
		Beautiful Conure
	cruentata	Blue-throated Conure
		Red-rumped Conure
		Red-eared Conure
		Ochre-marked Conure
	devillei	Blaze-winged Conure
		Deville's Conure
	egregia	Fiery-shouldered Conure
		Demerara Conure
	frontalis	Maroon-bellied Conure
		Red-bellied Conure
		Maroon Conure
		Brown-eared Conure
		Scaly-breasted Conure
	hoffmanni	Hoffmann's Conure
		Sulphur-winged Conure

Psittacidae Parrots, Lovebirds, Macaws (cont.)

	leucotis emma	Blue-naped Conure
		Emma's Conure
		Salvadori's Conure
	melanura	Maroon-tailed Conure
		Black-tailed Conure
	molinae	Green-cheeked Conure
		Molina's Conure
	picta	Painted Conure
		Blue-winged Conure
	rhodocephala	Rose-crowned Conure
		Rose-headed Conure
	rhodogaster	Crimson-bellied Conure
		Crimson-breasted Conure
		Rose-breasted Conure
		Rose-bellied Conure
	rupicola	Black-capped Conure
		Rock Conure
Enicognathus	*ferrugineus*	Austral Conure
		Emerald Conure
		Magellan Conure
	leptorhynchus	Slender-billed Conure
		Slight-billed Conure
		Long-billed Conure
Myiopsitta	*monachus*	Monk Parakeet
		Quaker Parakeet
		Grey-breasted Parakeet
Bolborhynchus	*aurifrons*	Mountain Parakeet
		Golden-fronted Parakeet★
	aymara	Sierra Parakeet
		Aymara Parakeet
		Grey-hooded Parakeet
		Andean Parakeet
	lineola	Barred Parakeet
		Lineolated Parakeet
		Catherine Parakeet
Forpus	*coelestis*	Celestial Parrotlet
		Pacific Parrotlet
		Lesson's Parrotlet
	cyanopygius	Mexican Parrotlet
		Blue-rumped Parrotlet

FAMILY/GENUS	SPECIES/SUBSPECIES	ENGLISH NAMES
		Turquoise-rumped Parrotlet
	passerinus	Green-rumped Parrotlet
		Green-and-blue-rumped Parrotlet
		Passerine Parrotlet
		Passerine Parrot
		Guiana Parrotlet
Brotogeris	*chrysopterus tuipara*	Golden-fronted Parakeet★
		Tuipara Parakeet
	cyanoptera	Cobalt-winged Parakeet
		Blue-winged Parakeet
		Deville's Parakeet
	jugularis	Orange-chinned Parakeet
		Tovi Parakeet
		Bee Bee Parakeet
	pyrrhopterus	Grey-cheeked Parakeet
		Orange-flanked Parakeet
		Orange-winged Parakeet
	sanctithomae	Tui Parakeet
		Golden-headed Parakeet
	tirica	Plain Parakeet
		All-green Parakeet
		Tirica Parakeet
	versicolorus	Canary-winged Parakeet
		Yellow-winged Parakeet
		White-winged Parakeet
Nannopsittaca	*panychlora*	Tepui Parrotlet
		Tepui Parakeet
		Mount Roraima Parakeet
Touit	*batavica*	Seven-coloured Parrotlet
		Black-winged Parrotlet
		Lilac-tailed Parrotlet
		Scopoli's Parrotlet
	dilectissima	
	dilectissima	Red-winged Parrotlet★
		Blue-fronted Parrotlet
		Mérida Parrotlet
	d. costaricensis	Red-fronted Parrotlet
		Costa Rica Parrotlet
	huetii	Scarlet-shouldered Parrotlet
		Red-winged Parrotlet★

Psittacidae Parrots, Lovebirds, Macaws (cont.)

		Huet's Parrotlet
	melanonota	Brown-backed Parrotlet
		Black-backed Parrotlet
		Wied's Parrotlet
	purpurata	Sapphire-rumped Parrotlet
		Purple Guiana Parrotlet
	stictoptera	Spot-winged Parrotlet
		Brown-shouldered Parrotlet
Pionites	*leucogaster*	White-bellied Caique
		White-breasted Caique
Pionopsitta	*barrabandi*	Barraband's Parrot
		Orange-cheeked Parrot
	caica	Caica Parrot
		Hooded Parrot
	haematotis	Brown-hooded Parrot
		Red-eared Parrot
	pileata	Pileated Parrot
		Red-capped Parrot*
	pulchra	Rose-faced Parrot
		Beautiful Parrot
	pyrilia	Saffron-headed Parrot
		Bonaparte's Parrot
Hapalopsittaca	*amazonina*	Rusty-faced Parrot
		Little Amazonian Parrot
		Bogota Parrot
	melanotis	Black-winged Parrot
		Black-eared Parrot
Pionus	*fuscus*	Dusky Parrot*
		Little Dusky Parrot
		Violet Parrot
		Violaceous Parrot
	maximiliani	Scaly-headed Parrot
		Maximilian's Parrot
	menstruus	Blue-headed Parrot
		Blue-hooded Parrot
		Red-vented Parrot
	senilis	White-capped Parrot
		White-crowned Parrot
	seniloides	White-headed Parrot
		Grey-headed Parrot

FAMILY/GENUS	SPECIES/SUBSPECIES	ENGLISH NAMES
		Massena's Parrot
	sordidus	Red-billed Parrot
		Sordid Parrot
		Dusky Parrot★
	tumultuosus	Plum-crowned Parrot
		Restless Parrot
		Tschudi's Parrot
Amazona	*agilis*	Black-billed Amazon Parrot
		All-green Amazon Parrot
		Active Amazon Parrot
	albifrons	White-fronted Amazon Parrot
		White-browed Amazon Parrot
		Spectacled Amazon Parrot
	arausiaca	Red-necked Amazon Parrot
		Bouquet's Amazon Parrot
		Dominican Blue-faced Amazon Parrot
		Lesser Dominican Amazon Parrot
	autumnalis	
	autumnalis	Red-lored Amazon Parrot
		Scarlet-lored Amazon Parrot
		Yellow-cheeked Amazon Parrot
		Primrose-cheeked Amazon Parrot
	a. lilacina	Lilacine Amazon Parrot
		Lesson's Amazon Parrot
	brasiliensis	Red-tailed Amazon Parrot
		Blue-faced Amazon Parrot
		Brazilian Green Amazon Parrot
	collaria	Yellow-billed Amazon Parrot
		Red-throated Amazon Parrot
		Jamaican Amazon Parrot
	dufresniana	
	dufresniana	Blue-cheeked Amazon Parrot
		Dufresne's Amazon Parrot
	d. rhodocorytha	Red-crowned Amazon Parrot
		Red-capped Amazon Parrot
		Red-topped Amazon Parrot
		Red-browed Amazon Parrot
	festiva	Festive Amazon Parrot
		Red-backed Amazon Parrot
	finschi	Lilac-crowned Amazon Parrot
		Finsch's Amazon Parrot

Psittacidae Parrots, Lovebirds, Macaws (cont.)

guildingii	St Vincent Amazon Parrot
	Guilding's Amazon Parrot
imperialis	Imperial Amazon Parrot
	August Amazon Parrot
	Dominican Amazon Parrot
leucocephala	Cuban Amazon Parrot
	White-headed Amazon Parrot
	Caribbean Amazon Parrot
mercenaria	Scaly-naped Amazon Parrot
	Scaly-naped Parrot
	Mercenary Amazon Parrot
	Tschudi's Amazon Parrot
ochrocephala	
ochrocephala	Yellow-crowned Amazon Parrot★
	Yellow-headed Amazon Parrot★
	Single Yellow-headed Amazon Parrot
	Yellow-fronted Amazon Parrot
o. oratrix	Double Yellow-headed Amazon Parrot
	Yellow-headed Amazon Parrot★
	Mexican Yellow-headed Amazon Parrot
	Double Yellow-fronted Amazon Parrot
	Levaillant's Amazon Parrot
pretrei	Red-spectacled Amazon Parrot
	Prêtre's Amazon Parrot
ventralis	Hispaniolan Amazon Parrot
	Salle's Amazon Parrot
	San Domingo Amazon Parrot
versicolor	St Lucia Amazon Parrot
	Versicoloured Amazon Parrot
	Blue-masked Amazon Parrot
vinacea	Vinaceous Amazon Parrot
	Vinaceous-breasted Amazon Parrot
viridigenalis	Green-cheeked Amazon Parrot
	Mexican Red-headed Parrot
	Red-crowned Parrot★
vittata	Puerto Rican Amazon Parrot
	Red-fronted Amazon Parrot

FAMILY/GENUS	SPECIES/SUBSPECIES	ENGLISH NAMES
	xanthops	Yellow-faced Amazon Parrot
		Yellow-crowned Amazon Parrot★
Deroptyus	*accipitrinus*	Hawk-headed Parrot
		Red Fan Parrot
		Hawk-headed Caique
Triclaria	*malachitacea*	Purple-bellied Parrot
		Purple-breasted Parrot
		Violet-bellied Parrot
		Blue-bellied Parrot

Musophagidae   Plantain-eaters, Turacos, Go-Away Birds
(All species alternatively known as Loeries/Louries.)

Tauraco	*hartlaubi*	Hartlaub's Turaco
		Blue-crested Turaco
	johnstoni	Ruwenzori Turaco
		Johnston's Turaco
	macrorhynchus	Crested Turaco
		Black-tipped Crested Turaco
		Great Billed Turaco
		Fraser's Turaco
		Verreaux's Turaco
	persa	Guinea Turaco
		Green Crested Turaco
		Green Loerie
		Gold Coast Turaco
		Senegal Turaco
	porphyreolophus	Violet-crested Turaco
		Purple-crested Turaco
Musophaga	*rossae*	Lady Ross's Turaco
		Ross's Turaco
		Ross's Violet Loerie
	violacea	Violet Turaco
		Violaceous Turaco
		Violaceous Plaintain-eater
		Violet Plaintain-eater
Corythaeola	*cristata*	Great Blue Turaco
		Blue Plaintain-eater
		Giant Plaintain-eater
Corythaixoides	*concolor*	Go-Away Bird
		Grey Turaco
		Grey Plaintain-eater

FAMILY/GENUS	SPECIES/SUBSPECIES	ENGLISH NAMES

Musophagidae Plantain-eaters, Turacos, Go-Away Birds (cont.)

	leucogaster	White-bellied Go-Away Bird
		White-bellied Turaco
	personata	Bare-faced Go-Away Bird
		Bare-faced Turaco
		Black-faced Loerie

Cuculidae Cuckoos, Roadrunner, Coucals

Clamator	*coromandus*	Red-winged Crested Cuckoo
		Chestnut-winged Cuckoo
	jacobinus	Jacobin Cuckoo
		Black and white Cuckoo
		Pied Crested Cuckoo
	levaillantii	Levaillant's Cuckoo
		Striped Crested Cuckoo
Cuculus	*canorus*	Cuckoo
		Grey Cuckoo
	fugax	Fugitive Hawk Cuckoo
		Hodgson's Hawk Cuckoo
	micropterus	Short-winged Cuckoo
		Indian Cuckoo
	poliocephalus	Eurasian Little Cuckoo
		Lesser Cuckoo
	saturatus	Oriental Cuckoo
		Blyth's Cuckoo
		Himalayan Cuckoo
	vagans	Lesser Hawk Cuckoo
		Moustached Cuckoo
	varius	Common Hawk Cuckoo
		Brainfever Bird
Cercococcyx	*mechowi*	Dusky Long-tailed Cuckoo
		Mechow's Cuckoo
	montanus	Barred Long-tailed Cuckoo
		Barred Cuckoo
	olivinus	Olive Long-tailed Cuckoo
		Olive Cuckoo
Cacomantis	*merulinus*	Grey-breasted Brush Cuckoo
		Plaintive Cuckoo*
	sonneratii	Banded Bay Cuckoo
		Bay-banded Cuckoo
Chrysococcyx	*basilis*	Horsfield's Bronze Cuckoo
		Horsfield's Cuckoo

FAMILY/GENUS	SPECIES/SUBSPECIES	ENGLISH NAMES
	crassirostris	Moluccan Bronze Cuckoo
		Island Cuckoo
	lucidus	Golden Bronze Cuckoo
		Shining Bronze Cuckoo
		Golden Cuckoo
Coccyzus	*minor*	Mangrove Cuckoo
		Black-eared Cuckoo
Saurothera	*merlini*	Great Lizard Cuckoo
		Cuban Lizard Cuckoo
Ceuthmochares	*aereus*	Yellow-bill
		Yellow-billed Cuckoo
		Green Coucal★
Morococcyx	*erythropygus*	Lesser Ground Cuckoo
		Rufous-rumped Ground Cuckoo
		Lesson's Ground Cuckoo
Dromococcyx	*pavoninus*	Pavonine Cuckoo
		Peacock Cuckoo
Geococcyx	*californianus*	Roadrunner
		Greater Roadrunner
Carpococcyx	*renauldi*	Coral-billed Ground Cuckoo
		Renauld's Ground Cuckoo
Coua	*serriana*	Red-breasted Coua
		Pucheran's Coua
Centropus	*ateralbus*	New Britain Coucal
		Pied Coucal
	bengalensis	Lesser Coucal
		Black Coucal
	bernsteinii	Bernstein's Coucal
		Bernstein's Ground Cuckoo
	leucogaster	Black-throated Coucal
		Great Coucal★
		Great Black-throated Coucal
	phasianinus	Pheasant Cuckoo
		Crow Pheasant★
	sinensis	Common Coucal
		Indian Coucal
		Crow Pheasant★
	viridis	Philippine Coucal
		Green Coucal★
Tytonidae Barn Owls		
Tyto	*alba*	Barn Owl
		White Owl

Tytonidae Barn Owls (cont.)

	inexpectata	Minahassa Barn Owl
		Unexpected Owl

Strigidae   Owls

Otus	*alfredi*	Flores Scops Owl
		Everett's Owl
	atricapillus	Long-tufted Screech Owl
		Black-capped Screech Owl
	brookei	Rajah's Scops Owl
		Rajah Brooke's Scops Owl
	choliba	Tropical Screech Owl
		Choliba Screech Owl
		Spix's Scops Owl
	icterorhynchus	Sandy Scops Owl
		Cinnamon Owl
	ireneae	Sokoke Scops Owl
		Mrs Morden's Owlet
	lawrencii	Bare-legged Owl
		Cuban Screech Owl
	leucotis	White-faced Scops Owl
		White-faced Owl
		White-faced Screech Owl
	spilocephalus	Spotted Scops Owl
		Mountain Scops Owl
	trichopsis	Whiskered Owl
		Spotted Screech Owl
Lophostrix	*letti*	Akun Scops Owl
		Maned Owl
Bubo	*bubo*	Great Eagle Owl
		Northern Eagle Owl
		Eagle Owl
	lacteus	Verreaux's Eagle Owl
		Milky Eagle Owl
		Giant Eagle Owl
	nipalensis	Forest Eagle Owl
		Spot-bellied Eagle Owl
	philippensis	Philippine Horned Owl
		Philippine Eagle Owl
	shelleyi	Banded Eagle Owl
		Shelley's Eagle Owl

FAMILY/GENUS	SPECIES/SUBSPECIES	ENGLISH NAMES
	sumatranus	Malay Eagle Owl
		Barred Eagle Owl
Ketupa	*ketupa*	Malay Fish Owl
		Javan Fish Owl
		Buffy Fish Owl
Pulsatrix	*koeniswaldiana*	Tawny-browed Owl
		White-chinned Owl
	melanota	Band-bellied Owl
		Rusty-barred Owl
Glaucidium	*brasilianum*	Ferruginous Pygmy Owl
		Streaked Pygmy Owl
	brodiei	Collared Pygmy Owl
		Collared Owlet
	cuculoides	Cuckoo Owl
		Cuckoo Owlet
		Asian Barred Owlet
	gnoma	Northern Pygmy Owl
		American Pygmy Owl
	passerinum	Eurasian Pygmy Owl
		Passerine Owl
Ninox	*connivens*	Barking Owl
		Winking Owl
	novaeseelandiae	Boobook Owl
		Spotted Owl
		Morepork
	solomonis	New Ireland Hawk Owl
		Carteret's Hawk Owl
Athene	*blewitti*	Forest Spotted Owlet
		Blewitt's Owl
	brama	Spotted Little Owl
		Spotted Owlet
Strix	*aluco*	Tawny Owl
		Brown Owl
		Wood Owl
Aegolius	*funereus*	Boreal Owl
		Tengmalm's Owl
		Richardson's Owl

Steatornithidae Oilbird

Steatornis	*caripensis*	Oilbird
		Diablotin*

FAMILY/GENUS	SPECIES/SUBSPECIES	ENGLISH NAMES

Caprimulgidae Nightjars

Lurocalis	*semitorquatus*	Semi-collared Nighthawk
		Short-tailed Nighthawk
Caprimulgus	*affinis*	Franklin's Nightjar
		Allied Nightjar
		Savannah Nightjar
	cayennensis	White-tailed Nightjar★
		Cayenne Nighthawk
	macrurus	Long-tailed Nightjar
		Large-tailed Nightjar
	natalensis	White-tailed Nightjar★
		Natal Nightjar
	nigrescens	Blackish Nightjar
		Dark Nighthawk
	pectoralis	Dusky Nightjar★
		Cuvier's Nightjar
		Fiery-necked Nightjar
	poliocephalus	Abyssinian Nightjar
		Rüppell's Nightjar
		Mountain Nightjar
	ridgwayi	Ridgway's Whip-poor-Will
		Buff-collared Nightjar
		Cookacheea
	saturatus	Dusky Nightjar★
		Sooty Nightjar
	tristigma	Freckled Nightjar
		Freckled Rock Nightjar

Apodidae Swifts

Chaetura	*boehmi*	Boehm's Spine-tailed Swift
		Bat-like Spinetail
Apus	*affinis*	House Swift
		Little Swift
	barbatus	African Black Swift
		Bearded Swift
	caffer	White-rumped Swift
		Caffer Swift
	pacificus	Northern White-rumped Swift
		Fork-tailed Swift
Panyptila	*cayennensis*	Lesser Swallow-tailed Swift
		Cayenne Swift

FAMILY/GENUS	SPECIES/SUBSPECIES	ENGLISH NAMES
	sanctihieronymi	Greater Swallow-tailed Swift
		Geronimo Swift
Trochilidae	Hummingbirds	
Tilmatura	*dupontii*	Sparkling-tailed Hummingbird
		Dupont's Hummingbird
Glaucis	*hirsuta*	Rufous-breasted Hermit
		Hairy Hermit
Threnetes	*leucurus*	Pale-tailed Barbthroat
		White-tailed Barbthroat
	ruckeri	Band-tailed Barbthroat
		Rucker's Barbthroat
Phaethornis	*anthophilus*	Pale-bellied Hermit
		Black-cheeked Hermit
	augusti	Sooty-capped Hermit
		Salle's Hermit
	bourcieri	Straight-billed Hermit
		Bourcier's Hermit
	gounellei	Broad-tipped Hermit
		Gounelle's Hermit
	griseogularis	Grey-chinned Hermit
		Grey-throated Hermit
	longuemareus	Little Hermit
		Dwarf Hermit
		Longuemare's Hermit
	malaris	Great-billed Hermit
		Nordmann's Hermit
	nattereri	Cinnamon-throated Hermit
		Natterer's Hermit
	squalidus	Dusky-throated Hermit
		Medium Hermit
	syrmatophorus	Tawny-bellied Hermit
		Train-bearing Hermit
	yaruqui	White-whiskered Hermit
		Black-winged Hermit
Eutoxeres	*aquila*	White-tipped Sicklebill
		Common Sicklebill
Phaeochroa	*cuvierii*	Scaly-breasted Hummingbird
		Cuvier's Hummingbird
Campylopterus	*ensipennis*	White-tailed Sabrewing
		Blue-throated Sabrewing

85

Trochilidae Hummingbirds (cont.)

	hemileucurus	Violet Sabrewing
		De Lattre's Sabrewing
Melanotrochilus	*fuscus*	Black Jacobin
		Black Hummingbird
Colibri	*coruscans*	Sparkling Violet-ear
		Gould's Violet-ear
Anthracothorax	*dominicus*	Antillean Mango
		Dominican Mango
	prevostii	Green-breasted Mango
		Prevost's Mango
Eulampis	*jugularis*	Purple-throated Carib
		Purple Carib
		Garnet-throated Hummingbird
Sericotes	*holosericeus*	Green-throated Carib
		Green Carib
Klais	*guimeti*	Violet-headed Hummingbird
		Violet-crowned Hummingbird
Abeillia	*abeillei*	Emerald-chinned Hummingbird
		Abeille's Hummingbird
Stephanoxis	*lalandi*	Black-breasted Plovercrest
		De Lalande's Plovercrest
		Plovercrest
Lophornis	*delattrei*	Rufous-crested Coquette
		De Lattre's Coquette
		De Lattre's Hummingbird
	gouldii	Dot-eared Coquette
		Gould's Coquette
Paphosia	*adorabilis*	White-crested Coquette
		Adorable Coquette
	helenae	Black-crested Coquette
		Princess Helena's Coquette
Popelairia	*langsdorffi*	Black-bellied Thorntail
		Black-breasted Thorntail
		Langsdorff's Thorntail
Discosura	*longicauda*	Racket-tailed Coquette
		Racket-tail
Chlorostilbon	*alice*	Green-tailed Emerald
		Alice's Emerald
	aureoventris	Glittering-bellied Emerald
		Glittering Emerald

FAMILY/GENUS	SPECIES/SUBSPECIES	ENGLISH NAMES
	canivetii	Fork-tailed Emerald
		Common Emerald
		Canivet's Emerald
	gibsoni	Red-billed Emerald
		Red-bellied Emerald
Thalurania	*furcata*	Fork-tailed Woodnymph
		Common Woodnymph
	watertonii	Long-tailed Woodnymph
		Waterton's Woodnymph
Panterpe	*insignis*	Fiery-throated Hummingbird
		Irazu Hummingbird
Damophila	*julie*	Violet-bellied Hummingbird
		Julie's Hummingbird
Hylocharis	*eliciae*	Blue-throated Goldentail
		Elicia's Goldentail
		Elicia's Hummingbird
	xantusii	Black-fronted Hummingbird
		Xantus's Hummingbird
Chrysuronia	*oenone*	Golden-tailed Sapphire
		Lesson's Sapphire
Amazilia	*amabilis*	Blue-chested Hummingbird
		Lovely Hummingbird
	amazilia	Amazilia Hummingbird
		Brown-bellied Amazilia
	cyanocephala	Red-billed Azurecrown
		Azure-crowned Hummingbird
	edward	Snowy-breasted Hummingbird
		White-bellied Hummingbird
	luciae	Honduras Emerald
		Lucy's Emerald
	rosenbergi	Purple-chested Hummingbird
		Rosenberg's Hummingbird
	saucerottei	Steely-vented Hummingbird
		Blue-vented Hummingbird
	tzacatl	Rufous-tailed Hummingbird
		Rieffer's Hummingbird
	yucatanensis	Buff-bellied Hummingbird
		Fawn-breasted Hummingbird
		Yucatan Hummingbird
Chalybura	*buffonii*	White-vented Plumeleteer
		Buffon's Plumeleteer

FAMILY/GENUS	SPECIES/SUBSPECIES	ENGLISH NAMES

Trochilidae Hummingbirds (cont.)

	urochrysia	Bronze-tailed Plumeleteer
		Gould's Plumeleteer
Lampornis	*amethystinus*	Amethyst-throated Hummingbird
		Cazique Hummingbird
	clemenciae	Blue-throated Hummingbird
		Blue-throated Sylph
		Blue-throated Mountain-gem
Heliodoxa	*gularis*	Pink-throated Brilliant
		Puce-throated Hummingbird
	imperatrix	Empress Brilliant
		Empress Eugene's Hummingbird
		Empress Hummingbird
	jacula	Green-crowned Brilliant
		Blue-throated Flying Dolphin
	leadbeateri	Violet-fronted Brilliant
		Blue-fronted Flying Dolphin
		Leadbeater's Brilliant
Eugenes	*fulgens*	Rivoli's Hummingbird
		Magnificent Hummingbird
Oreotrochilus	*estella*	Andean Hillstar
		Estella's Hillstar
Aglaeactis	*aliciae*	Purple-backed Sunbeam
		Alice's Sunbeam
Coeligena	*bonapartei*	Golden-bellied Starfrontlet
		Golden Starfrontlet
	torquata	Collared Inca
		Cavalier Hummingbird
	wilsoni	Brown Inca
		Wilson's Inca
		The King's Musketeer
Sephanoides	*sephanoides*	Green-backed Firecrown
		Chilean Firecrown
Heliangelus	*viola*	Purple-throated Sunangel
		Viola Sunangel
Eriocnemis	*cupreoventris*	Coppery-bellied Puffleg
		Copper-vented Puffleg
	derbyi	Black-thighed Puffleg
		Derby's Puffleg
Lesbia	*nuna*	Green-tailed Trainbearer
		Little Long-tailed Sylph

FAMILY/GENUS	SPECIES/SUBSPECIES	ENGLISH NAMES
	victoriae	Black-tailed Trainbearer
		Long-tailed Sylph
Sappho	*sparganura*	Red-tailed Comet
		Sappho Comet
Ramphomicron	*microrhynchum*	Purple-backed Thornbill
		Stanley's Thornbill
Metallura	*aeneocauda*	Scaled Metaltail
		Brassy Metaltail
Chalcostigma	*herrani*	Rainbow-bearded Thornbill
		Herran's Thornbill
	stanleyi	Blue-mantled Thornbill
		Stanley's Thornbill
Oxypogon	*guerinii*	Bearded Helmetcrest
		Linden's Helmetcrest
Opisthoprora	*euryptera*	Mountain Avocetbill
		Loddiges's Thornbill
Aglaiocercus	*coelestis*	Violet-tailed Sylph
		Heavenly Sylph
		Gould's Heavenly Sylph
	kingi	Long-tailed Sylph
		Blue-throated Sylph
		Blue-tailed Sylph
		Green-tailed Sylph
Schistes	*geoffroyi*	Wedge-billed Hummingbird
		Geoffrey's Wedgebill
Heliactin	*cornuta*	Horned Sungem
		Sungem
Loddigesia	*mirabilis*	Marvellous Spatuletail
		Loddiges's Spatuletail
		Loddiges's Raquet-tail
Heliomaster	*constanti*	Plain-capped Starthroat
		Constant's Starthroat
	furcifer	Blue-tufted Starthroat
		Angela Starthroat
	squamosus	Stripe-breasted Starthroat
		Brazilian Starthroat
Rhodopis	*vesper*	Oasis Hummingbird
		Evening Hummingbird
Thaumastura	*cora*	Peruvian Sheartail
		Cora Sheartail
Philodice	*bryantae*	Magenta-throated Woodstar

Trochilidae Hummingbirds (cont.)

		Costa Rican Woodstar
	mitchellii	Purple-throated Woodstar
		Mitchell's Woodstar
Microstilbon	*burmeisteri*	Slender-tailed Woodstar
		Burmeister's Woodstar
Atthis	*ellioti*	Elliot's Hummingbird
		Wine-throated Hummingbird
	heloisa	Bumblebee Hummingbird
		Heloize Hummingbird
Myrtis	*fanny*	Purple-collared Woodstar
		Fanny's Woodstar
Selasphorus	*flammula*	Rose-throated Hummingbird
		Rose-throated Flame-bearer
	scintilla	Scintillant Hummingbird
		Scintillant Flame-bearer
	simoni	Cerise-throated Hummingbird
		Simon's Hummingbird
	torridus	Heliotrope-throated Hummingbird
		Torrid Hummingbird

Coliidae   Mousebirds

(All species alternatively known as Mousebirds or Colies.)

Colius	*castanotus*	Red-backed Mousebird
		Chestnut-backed Mousebird
	striatus	Speckled Mousebird
		Striated Mousebird
		Bar-breasted Mousebird

Trogonidae   Trogons

Pharomachrus	*antisianus*	Crested Quetzal
		D'Orbigny's Trogon
	fulgidus	White-tipped Quetzal
		White-tipped Trogon
	mocinno	Resplendent Quetzal
		Quetzal
		Resplendent Trogon
	pavoninus	Golden-headed Quetzal
		Pavonine Trogon
Trogon	*collaris*	Collared Trogon
		Red-bellied Trogon
		Bar-tailed Trogon

FAMILY/GENUS	SPECIES/SUBSPECIES	ENGLISH NAMES
	curucui	Blue-crowned Trogon
		Purple-breasted Trogon
	elegans	Coppery-tailed Trogon
		Elegant Trogon
	massena	Slaty-tailed Trogon
		Massena Trogon
	mexicanus	Mountain Trogon
		Mexican Trogon
	rufus	Black-throated Trogon
		Graceful Trogon
	violaceus	Violaceous Trogon
		Gartered Trogon
Apaloderma	*aequatoriale*	Bare-cheeked Trogon
		Yellow-cheeked Trogon
Harpactes	*fasciatus*	Malabar Trogon
		Indian Trogon
		Ceylon Trogon
		Striped Trogon
	reinwardti	Reinwardt's Blue-tailed Trogon
		Blue-billed Trogon

Alcedinidae	Kingfishers	
Ceryle	*lugubris*	Greater Pied Kingfisher
		Crested Kingfisher
	rudis	Lesser Pied Kingfisher
		Pied Kingfisher
Alcedo	*euryzona*	Broad-zoned Kingfisher
		Blue-banded Kingfisher
	hercules	Blyth's Kingfisher
		Great Blue Kingfisher
	meninting	Blue-eared Kingfisher
		Deep-blue Kingfisher
Ceyx	*erithacus*	Three-toed Kingfisher
		Black-backed Kingfisher
	fallax	Celebes Pygmy Kingfisher
		Celebes Forest Kingfisher
	lecontei	African Dwarf Kingfisher
		Red-headed Pygmy Kingfisher
	lepidus	Dwarf Kingfisher
		Dwarf Forest Kingfisher
	melanurus	Philippine Forest Kingfisher

FAMILY/GENUS	SPECIES/SUBSPECIES	ENGLISH NAMES

Alcedinidae Kingfishers (cont.)

		Mindanao Kingfisher
	pusillus	African Mangrove Kingfisher
		Little Kingfisher
Dacelo	*novæguineae*	Laughing Kookaburra
		Laughing Jackass
		Kookaburra
	tyro	Aro Giant Kingfisher
		Tyro Kingfisher
Clytoceyx	*rex*	Shovel-billed Kingfisher
		Emperor Kingfisher
Halcyon	*albiventris*	Brown-hooded Kingfisher
		Brown-headed Kingfisher
	albonotata	White-backed Kingfisher
		New Britain Kingfisher
	australasia	Timor Kingfisher
		Australasian Kingfisher
	chloris	White-collared Kingfisher
		Mangrove Kingfisher
	cyanoventris	Java Kingfisher
		Blue-bellied Kingfisher
	fulgidus	Glittering Kingfisher
		Blue and White Kingfisher
	funebris	Sombre Kingfisher
		Funereal Kingfisher
	leucocephala	Grey-headed Kingfisher
		Chestnut-bellied Kingfisher
	megarhynchus	Mountain Yellow-billed Kingfisher
		Greater Yellow-billed Kingfisher
	monachus	Lonely Kingfisher
		Hooded Kingfisher
	princeps	Princely Kingfisher
		Mountain Kingfisher
	senegalensis	Woodland Kingfisher
		Angola Kingfisher
		Senegal Kingfisher
	smyrnensis	White-breasted Kingfisher
		Smyrna Kingfisher
	tuta	Borabora Kingfisher
		Respected Kingfisher
	venerata	Tahitian Kingfisher

FAMILY/GENUS	SPECIES/SUBSPECIES	ENGLISH NAMES
		Venerated Kingfisher
Tanysiptera	*galatea*	Common Paradise Kingfisher
		Beautiful Paradise Kingfisher
		Galatea Racket-tailed Kingfisher

Todidae Todies

Todus	*mexicanus*	Puerto Rican Tody
		Hypochondriac Tody

Momotidae Motmots

Eumomota	*superciliosa*	Turquoise-browed Motmot
		Yucatan Motmot
Momotus	*mexicanus*	Russet-crowned Motmot
		Mexican Motmot
	momota	Blue-crowned Motmot
		Brazilian Motmot

Meropidae Bee-eaters

Nyctyornis	*amicta*	Red-bearded Bee-eater
		Red-breasted Bee-eater
Merops	*leschenaulti*	Chestnut-headed Bee-eater
		Bay-headed Bee-eater
	orientalis	Little Green Bee-eater
		Green Bee-eater
	ornatus	Rainbow Bee-eater
		Rainbow Bird
		Australian Bee-eater
	superciliosus	Blue-cheeked Bee-eater
		Blue-tailed Bee-eater
		Brown-breasted Bee-eater
	variegatus	Blue-breasted Bee-eater
		White-cheeked Bee-eater

Leptosomatidae Courol

Leptosomus	*discolor*	Kirombo Coural
		Coural
		Cuckoo Roller

Coraciidae Rollers

Coracias	*abyssinica*	Abyssinian Roller

FAMILY/GENUS	SPECIES/SUBSPECIES	ENGLISH NAMES

Coraciidae Rollers (cont.)

		Senegal Roller
	benghalensis	Indian Roller
		Indian Blue Roller
	caudata	Lilac-breasted Roller
		Fork-tailed Roller
	garrulus	Blue Roller
		Common Roller
		European Roller
		Roller
	naevia	Rufous-crowned Roller
		Purple Roller
Eurystomus	*glaucurus*	African Broad-billed Roller
		Cinnamon Roller
	orientalis	Broad-billed Roller
		Oriental Broad-billed Roller
		Dollarbird
		Oriental Dollarbird

Phoeniculidae Wood Hoopoes

Phoeniculus	*aterrimus*	Black Wood Hoopoe
		Lesser Wood Hoopoe
	purpureus	Green Wood Hoopoe
		Senegal Wood Hoopoe
		Red-billed Wood Hoopoe

Bucerotidae Hornbills

Tockus	*erythrorhynchus*	Red-billed Hornbill
		Red-beaked Hornbill
	fasciatus	Pied Hornbill
		African Pied Hornbill
		Black-and-white-tailed Hornbill
Berenicornis	*comatus*	Asiatic White-crested Hornbill
		White-crowned Hornbill
Ptilolaemus	*tickelli*	White-throated Brown Hornbill
		Brown Hornbill
Penelopides	*exarhatus*	Temminck's Hornbill
		Celebes Hornbill★
	panini	Rufous-tailed Hornbill
		Tarictic Hornbill
Aceros	*cassidix*	Celebes Hornbill★

94

		Buton Hornbill
	leucocephalus	Wrinkled Hornbill
		Writhe-billed Hornbill
	plicatus	Blyth's Hornbill
		Papuan Hornbill
	undulatus	Wreathed Hornbill
		Plait-billed Hornbill
Anthracoceros	*coronatus*	Malabar Pied Hornbill
		Crowned Hornbill
	marchei	Palawan Hornbill
		Marche's Hornbill
	montani	Sulu Hornbill
		Montano's Hornbill
Bycanistes	*brevis*	Silver-cheeked Hornbill
		Crested Hornbill
	subcylindricus	Black and White Casqued Hornbill
		Casqued Hornbill
		Grey-cheeked Hornbill
Buceros	*bicornis*	Great Pied Hornbill
		Great Hornbill
		Giant Hornbill
		Indian Hornbill
		Concave-casqued Hornbill
	hydrocorax	Rufous Hornbill
		Philippine Hornbill
		Calao
Bucorvus	*abyssinicus*	Abyssinian Ground Hornbill
		North African Ground Hornbill
		African Ground Hornbill
	cafer	Southern Ground Hornbill
		Kaffir Hornbill

Galbulidae Jacamars
| *Galbula* | *ruficauda* | Rufous-tailed Jacamar |
| | | Black-faced Jacamar |

Capitonidae Barbets
Capito	*aurovirens*	Scarlet-crowned Barbet
		Plaintive Barbet
	squamatus	Orange-fronted Barbet
		Rufous-fronted Barbet

FAMILY/GENUS	SPECIES/SUBSPECIES	ENGLISH NAMES

Capitonidae Barbets (cont.)

Eubucco	*bourcierii*	Red-headed Barbet
		Flame-headed Barbet
		Bourcier's Barbet
Semnornis	*ramphastinus*	Toucan Barbet
		Toucan-billed Barbet
Megalaima	*asiatica*	Blue-throated Barbet
		Blue-cheeked Barbet
	australis	Blue-eared Barbet
		Little Barbet
	flavifrons	Yellow-fronted Barbet
		Yellow-faced Barbet
	haemacephala	Crimson-breasted Barbet
		Crimson-headed Barbet
		Coppersmith Barbet
		Coppersmith
	incognita	Hume's Blue-throated Barbet
		Moustached Barbet
	javensis	Black-banded Barbet
		Kotorea Barbet
	lagrandieri	Red-vented Barbet
		Lagrandier's Barbet
	mystacophanes	Gaudy Barbet
		Red-throated Barbet
	oorti	Muller's Barbet
		Black-browed Barbet
		Embroidered Barbet
	pulcherrima	Golden-naped Barbet
		Golden-rumped Barbet
		Kinabalu Barbet
	rafflesii	Many-coloured Barbet
		Red-crowned Barbet
	rubricapilla	Crimson-throated Barbet
		Small Barbet
	virens	Great Barbet
		Giant Barbet
		Giant Hill Barbet
	zeylanica	Oriental Green Barbet
		Green Barbet*
		Brown-headed Barbet
		Lineated Barbet

FAMILY/GENUS	SPECIES/SUBSPECIES	ENGLISH NAMES
Pogoniulus	*bilineatus*	Golden-rumped Tinkerbird
		Lemon-rumped Tinkerbird
	chrysoconus	Yellow-fronted Tinkerbird
		Yellow-fronted Barbet
	makawai	Black-chinned Tinkerbird
		White-chested Tinkerbird
	pusillus	Red-fronted Tinkerbird
		Red-fronted Tinker Barbet
Lybius	*bidentatus*	Double-tooth Barbet
		Tooth-billed Barbet
		Groove-billed Barbet★
	dubius	Bearded Barbet
		Groove-billed Barbet★
	hirsutus	Hairy-breasted Barbet
		Hairy-breasted Toothbill
	melanocephalum	African Black-throated Barbet
		Brown-throated Barbet
Trachyphonus	*margaritatus*	Yellow-breasted Barbet
		Abyssinian Barbet
	vaillantii	Levaillant's Barbet
		Levaillant's Ground Barbet
		Crested Barbet
		Black-backed Barbet

Indicatoridae	Honeyguides	
Prodotiscus	*insignis*	Cassin's Honeybird
		Cassin's Sharp-billed Honeyguide
	regulus	Wahlberg's Honeybird
		Brown-backed Honeyguide
Indicator	*indicator*	Black-throated Honeyguide
		Greater Honeyguide
	pumilio	Pygmy Honeyguide
		Dwarf Honeyguide
	xanthonotus	Indian Honeyguide
		Yellow-rumped Honeyguide

Ramphastidae	Toucans	
Aulacorhynchus	*haematopygus*	Crimson-rumped Toucan
		Crimson-rumped Aracari
		Red-rumped Green Toucanet
		Chestnut-billed Emerald Toucanet

FAMILY/GENUS	SPECIES/SUBSPECIES	ENGLISH NAMES

Ramphastidae Toucans (cont.)

(All species of genus *Pteroglossus* alternatively known as Toucans or Aracaris.)

Pteroglossus	*aracari*	Black-necked Aracari
		Maximilian's Aracari
	bitorquatus	Red-necked Aracari
		Double-collared Aracari
	erythropygius	Pale-mandibled Aracari
		Red-rumped Aracari
		Scarlet-rumped Aracari
		Red-backed Aracari
	flavirostris	Ivory-billed Aracari
		Yellow-billed Aracari
	mariae	Brown-mandibled Aracari
		Maria's Toucan
	torquatus	Collared Aracari
		Banded Aracari
		Ringed Aracari
Selenidera	*nattereri*	Tawny-tufted Toucanet
		Natterer's Toucanet
	reinwardtii	Golden-collared Toucanet
		Reinwardt's Toucanet
Andigena	*bailloni*	Saffron Toucanet
		Baillon's Toucan
		Banana Toucan
	laminirostris	Plate-billed Mountain Toucan
		Laminated Hill Toucan
		Laminated-billed Toucan
Ramphastos	*dicolorus*	Red-breasted Toucan
		Green-billed Toucan
	sulfuratus	Keel-billed Toucan
		Sulphur-breasted Toucan
		Rainbow-billed Toucan
	swainsonii	Chestnut-mandibled Toucan
		Swainson's Toucan
	toco	Toco Toucan
		Giant Toucan
	vitellinus	Channel-billed Toucan
		Sulphur-and-white-breasted Toucan

Picidae   Woodpeckers, Piculets

(All species of genus *Picumnus* alternatively known as Piculets or Woodpeckers.

Colaptes	*auratus*	Common Flicker
		Yellow-shafted Flicker
		Golden-winged Woodpecker
	campestris	Campo Flicker
		Campos Flicker
		Pampas Flicker
	fernandinae	Fernandina's Flicker
		Cuba Flicker
Piculus	*auricularis*	Grey-crowned Woodpecker
		Western Green Woodpecker
	rubiginosus	Golden-olive Woodpecker
		Green Woodpecker*
		Swainson's Woodpecker
Campethera	*cailliautii*	Little Spotted Woodpecker
		Green-backed Woodpecker
	caroli	Brown-eared Woodpecker
		Buff-spotted Woodpecker
Celeus	*elegans*	Chestnut Woodpecker
		Elegant Woodpecker
Picus	*canus*	Grey-headed Woodpecker
		Ashy Woodpecker
	erythropygius	Red-rumped Green Woodpecker
		Black-headed Woodpecker
	viridanus	Burmese Scaly-bellied Woodpecker
		Streak-breasted Woodpecker
Dinopium	*benghalense*	Lesser Golden-backed Woodpecker
		Black-rumped Goldenback
		Golden-backed Woodpecker
	javanense	Golden-backed Three-toed Woodpecker
		Common Goldenback
		Greater Golden-backed Woodpecker*
	rafflesii	Olive-backed Three-toed Woodpecker
		Olive-backed Woodpecker
		Raffle's Woodpecker
	shorii	Himalayan Three-toed Woodpecker
		Himalayan Goldenback
		Himalayan Golden-backed Woodpecker

FAMILY/GENUS	SPECIES/SUBSPECIES	ENGLISH NAMES

Picidae Woodpeckers, Piculets (cont.)

Meiglyptes	*tristis*	Fulvous-rumped Barred Woodpecker
		Buff-rumped Woodpecker
Dryocopus	*lineatus*	Lineated Woodpecker
		White-bellied Woodpecker
	martius	Black Woodpecker
		Great Black Woodpecker
Phloeoceastes	*guatemalensis*	Pale-bellied Woodpecker
		Pale-billed Woodpecker
		Flint-billed Woodpecker
		Guatemalan Ivory-billed Woodpecker
Leuconerpes	*candidus*	White Woodpecker
		White-headed Woodpecker
Melanerpes	*formicivorus*	Acorn Woodpecker
		Ant-eating Woodpecker
		California Woodpecker
	hypopolius	Grey-breasted Woodpecker
		Balsas Woodpecker
		Desert Woodpecker
		Gila Woodpecker
	pucherani	Black-cheeked Woodpecker
		Pucheran's Woodpecker
		White-barred Woodpecker
	rubricapillus	Red-crowned Woodpecker
		Wagler's Woodpecker
		Red-vented Woodpecker
Sphyrapicus	*thyroideus*	Williamson's Sapsucker
		Black-crowned Sapsucker
	varius	Yellow-bellied Sapsucker
		Red-naped Sapsucker
		Common Sapsucker
Veniliornis	*affinis*	Red-stained Woodpecker
		Stained Woodpecker
	dignus	Yellow-fronted Woodpecker
		Yellow-vented Woodpecker
	fumigatus	Smoky-brown Woodpecker
		Smoky Woodpecker
		Smoke-coloured Woodpecker
		Oleaginous Woodpecker
Picoides	*arcticus*	Black-headed Three-toed Woodpecker

FAMILY/GENUS	SPECIES/SUBSPECIES	ENGLISH NAMES
		Arctic Woodpecker
		Arctic Three-toed Woodpecker
	canicapillus	Grey-headed Pygmy Woodpecker
		Grey-capped Woodpecker
	cathpharius	Lesser Pied Woodpecker
		Crimson-breasted Woodpecker
		Asian Spotted Woodpecker
	mahrattensis	Yellow-fronted Pied Woodpecker
		Yellow-crowned Woodpecker
		Mahratta Woodpecker
	medius	Middle Spotted Woodpecker
		Medium Spotted Woodpecker
	moluccensis	Brown-capped Pied Woodpecker
		Malaysian Pygmy Woodpecker
	scalaris	Ladder-backed Woodpecker
		Cactus Woodpecker
	stricklandi	Brown-backed Woodpecker
		Brown-barred Woodpecker
	tridactylus	Three-toed Woodpecker
		Northern Three-toed Woodpecker
Sapheopico	*noguchii*	Pryer's Woodpecker
		Okinawa Woodpecker
Mesopicos	*griseocephalus*	African Grey-headed Woodpecker
		Olive Woodpecker
	xantholophus	Yellow-crested Woodpecker
		Golden-crowned Woodpecker
Hemicircus	*concretus*	Malaysian Grey-breasted Woodpecker
		Grey and Buff Woodpecker
Blythipicus	*rubiginosus*	Lesser Bay Woodpecker
		Maroon Woodpecker
Chrysocolaptes	*festivus*	Black-backed Woodpecker
		White-naped Woodpecker
	lucidus	Crimson-backed Woodpecker
		Greater Goldenback*
Eurylaimidae	Broadbills	
Smithornis	*capensis*	Delacour's Broadbill
		Black-capped Broadbill
		African Broadbill
	rufolateralis	Rufous-sided Broadbill

Eurylaimidae Broadbills (cont.)

		Red-sided Broadbill
	sharpei	Grey-headed Broadbill
		Sharpe's Broadbill
Serilophus	*lunatis*	Silver-breasted Broadbill
		Collared Broadbill
Calyptomena	*viridis*	Lesser Green Broadbill
		Green Broadbill*

Dendrocolaptidae Wood-creepers

(Many species alternatively known as Wood-creepers or Creepers.)

Glyphorhynchus	*spirurus*	Wedge-billed Wood-creeper
		Wedgebill
Xiphocolaptes	*promeropirhynchus*	Strong-billed Wood-creeper
		Great-billed Wood-creeper
Dendrocolaptes	*certhia*	Barred Wood-creeper
		Barred Wood-hewer
Xiphorhynchus	*erythropygius*	Spotted Wood-creeper
		Spotted Wood-hewer
	flavigaster	Ivory-billed Wood-creeper
		Ivory-billed Wood-hewer
Lepidocolaptes	*affinis*	Spot-crowned Wood-creeper
		Allied Wood-creeper
		Allied Wood-hewer
	leucogaster	White-striped Wood-creeper
		White-bellied Creeper
	souleyetii	Streak-headed Wood-creeper
		Thin-billed Wood-hewer
		Souleyet's Creeper

Furnariidae Ovenbirds

(All species of genus *Furnarius* alternatively known as Ovenbirds or
Horneros.)

Furnarius	*figulus*	Wing-banded Hornero
		Banded Ovenbird
	rufus	Rufous Hornero
		Ovenbird*

(Many species of genera *Anabacerthia, Philydor, Automolus* and *Hylocryptus*
alternatively known as Foliage-gleaners or Leaf-gleaners.)

Anabacerthia	*striaticollis*	Montane Foliage-gleaner
		Scaly-throated Foliage-gleaner
		Scaly-throated Tree-hunter

FAMILY/GENUS	SPECIES/SUBSPECIES	ENGLISH NAMES
Automolus	*rubiginosus*	Ruddy Foliage-gleaner
		Ruddy-throated Automolus
		Ruddy Ovenbird
Xenops	*minutus*	Plain Xenops
		Little Xenops
Sclerurus	*mexicanus*	Tawny-throated Leaf-scraper
		Mexican Leaf-scraper
	guatemalensis	Scaly-throated Leaf-scraper
		Guatemalan Leaf-scraper

Formicariidae   Antbirds

Thamnophilus	*torquatus*	Rufous-winged Ant-shrike
		Ringed Ant-shrike
Pygiptila	*stellaris*	Spot-winged Ant-shrike
		Starred Ant-shrike
Xenornis	*setifrons*	Speckle-breasted Ant-shrike
		Spiny-faced Ant-shrike
Thamnistes	*anabatinus*	Russet Ant-shrike
		Tawny Bush Bird
Dysithamnus	*puncticeps*	Spot-crowned Ant-vireo
		Spotted Ant-vireo
	striaticeps	Streak-crowned Ant-vireo
		Streaked Ant-vireo
Myrmotherula	*axillaris*	White-flanked Ant-wren
		Black Ant-wren
	erythronotos	Black-hooded Ant-wren
		Hooded Ant-wren
	fulviventris	Checker-throated Ant-wren
		Chequered Ant-wren
		Fulvous Ant-wren
Microrhopias	*quixensis*	Dot-winged Ant-wren
		Velvety Ant-wren
Formicarius	*analis*	Black-faced Ant-thrush
		Chestnut-collared Ant-thrush
Pithys	*albifrons*	White-plumed Antbird
		White-faced Antbird
Grallaricula	*ferrugineipectus*	Rusty-breasted Ant-pitta
		Rusty Ant-pitta
	flavirostris	Ochre-breasted Ant-pitta
		Ochraceous Ant-pitta
	nana	Slate-crowned Ant-pitta

FAMILY/GENUS	SPECIES/SUBSPECIES	ENGLISH NAMES

Formicariidae Antbirds (cont.)

		Crowned Ant-pitta
Grallaria	*dignissima*	Ochre-striped Ant-pitta
		Striped Ant-pitta
	hypoleuca	Bay-backed Ant-pitta
		White-bellied Ant-pitta
	varia	Variegated Ant-pitta
		Antbird
		Royal Ant-thrush

Pittidae Pittas

(All species alternatively known as Jewel-thrushes and Ant-thrushes, but latter is also name of members of Formicariidae.)

Pitta	*brachyura*	Blue-winged Pitta*
		Green-winged Pitta [1]
		Indian Pitta
		Bengal Pitta
		Fairy Pitta
	caerulea	Great Blue Pitta
		Giant Pitta
	cyanea	Lesser Blue Pitta
		Blue Pitta
	ellioti	Bar-bellied Pitta
		Elliot's Pitta
	erythrogaster	Red-breasted Pitta
		Blue-breasted Pitta [1]
	guajana	Blue-tailed Pitta
		Banded Pitta
		Irene Pitta
		Van den Bock's Pitta
	iris	Rainbow Pitta
		Black-breasted Pitta
	maxima	Halmahera Pitta
		Great Pitta
	moluccensis	Moluccan Pitta
		Blue-winged Pitta*
	oatesi	Fulvous Pitta
		Rusty-naped Pitta
	phayrei	Phayre's Pitta
		Eared Pitta

[1] Colour variable through range.

	sordida	Black-headed Pitta
		Hooded Pitta
	soror	Blue-backed Pitta
		Blue-rumped Pitta

Tyrannidae Tyrant Flycatchers

Agriornis	*livida*	Great Shrike Tyrant
		Kittlitz's Shrike Tyrant
Neoxolmis	*rufiventris*	Chocolate-vented Tyrant
		Chocolate Tyrant
Xolmis	*dominicana*	Black and White Monjita
		Dominican Monjita
	irupero	White Monjita
		Widow Monjita
	murina	Mouse-brown Monjita
		Brown Monjita
	rubetra	Rusty-backed Monjita
		Chat-like Monjita
	velata	White-rumped Monjita
		Veiled Monjita
Muscisaxicola	*albilora*	White-browed Ground Tyrant
		White-lored Ground Tyrant
	alpina	Plain-capped Ground Tyrant
		Cinerous Ground Tyrant
		Alpine Ground Tyrant
	capistrata	Cinnamon-bellied Ground Tyrant
		Burmeister's Ground Tyrant
Ochthoeca	*diadema*	Yellow-bellied Chat Tyrant
		Hartlaub's Chat Tyrant
Knipolegus	*nigerrimus*	Velvety Black Tyrant
		Vieillot's Black Tyrant
	orenocensis	Riverside Tyrant
		Orinoco Tyrant
	poecilocercus	Amazonian Black Tyrant
		Pelzeln's Black Tyrant
Pyrocephalus	*rubinus*	Vermilion Flycatcher
		Scarlet Flycatcher
Tumbezia	*salvini*	Tumbes Tyrant
		Salvin's Tyrant
Machetornis	*rixosus*	Cattle Tyrant
		Cattle Flycatcher

FAMILY/GENUS	SPECIES/SUBSPECIES	ENGLISH NAMES

Tyrannidae Tyrant Flycatchers (cont.)

		Fire-crowned Tyrant
Tyrannus	*caudifasciatus*	Loggerhead Kingbird
		Petchary
	melancholicus	Tropical Kingbird
		Azara's Kingbird
		Melancholy Kingbird
Empidonomus	*aurantioatrocristatus*	Variegated Flycatcher
		Varied Flycatcher
Legatus	*leucophaius*	Piratic Flycatcher
		Striped Flycatcher
Myiozetetes	*similis*	Social Flycatcher
		Vermilion-crowned Flycatcher
Attila	*spadiceus*	Bright-rumped Attila
		Polymorphic Attila
		Mexican Attila
Pitangus	*sulphuratus*	Great Kiskadee
		Sulphury Tyrant
		Derby Flycatcher
		Derbian Flycatcher
		Kiskadee Flycatcher
Myiarchus	*barbirostris*	Jamaican Flycatcher
		Sad Flycatcher
	nuttingi	Pale-throated Flycatcher
		Nutting's Flycatcher
	phaeocephalus	Sooty-crowned Flycatcher
		Ashy-fronted Flycatcher
	tuberculifer	Dusky-capped Flycatcher
		Olivaceous Flycatcher
	tyrannulus	Wied's Crested Flycatcher
		Wied's Flycatcher
		Brown-crested Flycatcher
Contopus	*cinereus*	Tropical Pewee
		Ash-coloured Pewee
	fumigatus	Greater Pewee★
		Smoky Pewee
	pertinax	Coues's Flycatcher
		Greater Pewee★
Empidonax	*affinis*	Pine Flycatcher
		Allied Flycatcher
	alnorum	Alder Flycatcher★

FAMILY/GENUS	SPECIES/SUBSPECIES	ENGLISH NAMES
		Traill's Flycatcher★
	fulvifrons	Buff-breasted Flycatcher
		Fulvous Flycatcher
		Ruddy Flycatcher
	oberholseri	Dusky Flycatcher
		Wright's Flycatcher
	traillii	Willow Flycatcher
		Traill's Flycatcher★
		Alder Flycatcher★
Xenotriccus	*callizonus*	Belted Flycatcher
		Cinnamon-breasted Flycatcher
Aphanotriccus	*audax*	Black-billed Flycatcher
		Nelson's Flycatcher
	capitalis	Tawny-chested Flycatcher
		Salvin's Flycatcher
Platyrinchus	*mystaceus*	White-throated Spadebill
		Stub-tailed Spadebill
		White-throated Flatbill
Tolmomyias	*assimilis*	Yellow-margined Flycatcher
		Similar Flycatcher
	sulphurescens	Yellow-olive Flycatcher
		White-eyed Flycatcher
		Sulphury Flatbill
Rhynchocyclus	*brevirostris*	Eye-ringed Flatbill
		Short-tailed Flatbill

(All species of genus *Todirostrum* alternatively known as Tody Tyrants or Tody Flycatchers.)

Todirostrum	*plumbeiceps*	Ochre-faced Tody Flycatcher
		Lead-Crowned Tody Tyrant
	sylvia	Slate-headed Tody Flycatcher
		Desmarest's Tody Tyrant
Elaenia	*obscura*	Highland Elaenia
		Dusky Elaenia
Camptostoma	*imberbe*	Beardless Flycatcher
		Northern Beardless Flycatcher
		Beardless Tyrannulet
		Northern Beardless Tyrannulet
	obsoletum	Southern Beardless Tyrannulet
		Southern Beardless Flycatcher
Phyllomyias	*griseiceps*	Sooty-headed Tyrannulet
		Crested Tyrannulet

FAMILY/GENUS	SPECIES/SUBSPECIES	ENGLISH NAMES

Tyrannidae Tyrant Flycatchers (cont.)

Ornithion	*inerme*	White-lored Tyrannulet
		Hartlaub's Tyrannulet
Pipromorpha	*oleaginea*	Ochre-bellied Flycatcher
		Oleagineous Flycatcher
	rufiventris	Grey-hooded Flycatcher
		Rufous-bellied Flycatcher

Pipridae   Manakins

Pipra	*iris*	Opal-crowned Manakin
		Pearl-headed Manakin
	mentalis	Red-capped Manakin
		Red-headed Manakin
		Yellow-thighed Manakin
Teleonema	*filicauda*	Wire-tailed Manakin
		Cirrhate Manakin
Chiroxiphia	*lanceolata*	Sharp-tailed Manakin
		Lance-tailed Manakin
	pareola	Blue-backed Manakin
		Superb Manakin
Ilicura	*militaris*	Pin-tailed Manakin
		Military Manakin
Corapipo	*leucorrhoa*	White-ruffed Manakin
		White-bibbed Manakin
Manacus	*manacus*	White-bearded Manakin
		Black and White Manakin
		Edward's Manakin
	vitellinus	Golden-collared Manakin
		Gould's Manakin
Chloropipo	*uniformis*	Olive Manakin
		Uniform Manakin
Piprites	*pileatus*	Black-capped Manakin
		Pileated Manakin
Schiffornis	*turdinus*	Thrush-like Manakin
		Brown Manakin

Cotingidae   Cotingas, Cocks-of-the-Rock, Becards

Rupicola	*peruviana*	Andean Cock-of-the-Rock
		Red Cock-of-the-Rock
	rupicola	Guianan Cock-of-the-Rock

FAMILY/GENUS	SPECIES/SUBSPECIES	ENGLISH NAMES
		Golden Cock-of-the-Rock
		Orange Cock-of-the-Rock
Carpornis	*cucullatus*	Hooded Berry-eater
		Hooded Cotinga
	melanocephalus	Black-headed Berry-eater
		Black-headed Cotinga
Cotinga	*cayana*	Spangled Cotinga
		Purple-throated Cotinga
	maculata	Banded Cotinga
		Spotted Cotinga
		Banded Chatterer
	maynana	Plum-throated Cotinga
		Mayna's Cotinga
	ridgwayi	Turquoise Cotinga
		Ridgway's Cotinga
Xipholena	*atropurpurea*	White-winged Cotinga
		Wied's Cotinga
	lamellipennis	White-tailed Cotinga
		Lafresnaye's Cotinga
Carpodectes	*antoniae*	Yellow-billed Cotinga
		Antonia's Cotinga
Ampelion	*sclateri*	Bay-vented Cotinga
		Sclater's Cotinga

(All species of genus *Pipreola* alternatively known as Cotingas or Fruit-eaters.)

FAMILY/GENUS	SPECIES/SUBSPECIES	ENGLISH NAMES
Pipreola	*pulchra*	Masked Fruit-eater
		Beautiful Fruit-eater
	riefferii	Green and Black Fruit-eater
		Black-throated Cotinga
Iodopleura	*isabellae*	White-browed Purpletuft
		Isabella's Cotinga
	pipra	Buff-throated Purpletuft
		Lesson's Cotinga
Pachyramphus	*castaneus*	Chestnut-crowned Becard
		Rufous Becard
	major	Grey-collared Becard
		Black-capped Becard
		Mexican Becard
Tityra	*cayana*	Black-tailed Tityra
		Cayenne Tityra
	inquisitor	Black-crowned Tityra

Cotingidae Cotingas, Cocks-of-the-Rock, Becards (cont.)

		Black-capped Tityra
		Inquisitor Tityra
Cephalopterus	*ornatus*	Amazonian Umbrellabird
		Ornate Umbrellabird
Perisso͞ ͡phalus	*tricolor*	Capuchinbird
		Calfbird
Procnias	*averano*	Bearded Bellbird
		Mossy-throated Bellbird
		Black-winged Bellbird
	nudicollis	Bare-throated Bellbird
		Naked-throated Bellbird

Menuridae   Lyrebirds

Menura	*alberti*	Albert's Lyrebird
		Prince Albert's Lyrebird

Atrichornithidae   Scrub-birds

Atrichornis	*clamosus*	Noisy Scrub-bird
		Western Scrub-bird

Alaudidae   Larks

(Many species of genus *Mirafra* alternatively known as Larks or Bush Larks.)

Mirafra	*cheniana*	Southern Singing Bush Lark
		Latakoo Lark
	javanica	Singing Bush Lark
		White-tailed Bush Lark
	nigricans	Dusky Lark
		Rufous-rumped Bush Lark
	williamsi	Marsabit Lark
		William's Lark
Eremopterix	*leucotis*	Chestnut-backed Finch Lark
		White-cheeked Finch Lark
Ammomanes	*cincturus*	Bar-tailed Desert Lark
		Bar-tailed Sand Lark
		Black-tailed Sand Lark
	phoenicurus	Rufous-tailed Finch Lark
		Rufous-tailed Lark
		Rufous-tailed Desert Lark
Alaemon	*alaudipes*	Bifasciated Lark

FAMILY/GENUS	SPECIES/SUBSPECIES	ENGLISH NAMES
		Hoopoe Lark
		Greater Hoopoe Lark
Rhamphocoris	*clot-bey*	Thick-billed Lark
		Clotbey Lark
Melanocorypha	*bimaculata*	Eastern Calandra Lark
		Bimaculated Lark
Calandrella	*cinerea*	Short-toed Lark
		Red-capped Lark
	raytal	Sand Lark
		Raytal Lark
	sclateri	Sclater's Short-toed Lark
		Sclater's Lark
	starki	Stark's Short-toed Lark
		Stark's Lark
Galerida	*deva*	Syke's Crested Lark
		Deccan Lark
	modesta	Sun Lark
		Nigerian Crested Lark
Alauda	*gulgula*	Small Skylark
		Lesser Skylark
Eremophila	*alpestris*	Horned Lark
		Shore Lark
	bilopha	Temminck's Horned Lark
		Temminck's Lark
Hirundinidae	Swallows, Martins	
Progne	*chalybea*	Grey-breasted Martin
		White-bellied Martin★
	dominicensis	Caribbean Martin
		White-bellied Martin★
Atticora	*fasciata*	White-banded Swallow
		White-backed Swallow
Stelgidopteryx	*ruficollis*	Rough-winged Swallow
		Galley Martin
Cheramoeca	*leucosterna*	White-backed Swallow
		Black and White Swallow
Riparia	*paludicola*	Brown-throated Sand Martin
		Plain Sand Martin
		African Sand Martin
	riparia	Bank Swallow
		Sand Martin

Hirundinidae Swallows, Martins (cont.)

Hirundo	*daurica*	Red-rumped Swallow
		Daurian Swallow
	nigrita	Little Blue Swallow
		White-throated Blue Swallow
	nigroufa	Congo Swallow
		Black and Red Swallow
		Black and Rufous Swallow
	rustica	Barn Swallow
		Swallow
	semirufa	Rufous-chested Swallow
		Red-breasted Swallow
	striolata	Striated Swallow
		Oriental Mosque Swallow

(All species of genus *Psalidoprocne* alternatively known as Rough-winged
Swallows or Saw-wings.)

Motacillidae Wagtails, Pipits

Motacilla	*citreola*	Yellow-headed Wagtail
		Yellow-hooded Wagtail
		Citrine Wagtail
	clara	Mountain Wagtail
		Long-tailed Wagtail
Anthus	*antarctica*	Sub-antarctic Pipit
		South Georgia Pipit
	caffer	Bushveld Tree Pipit
		Little Pipit
	hodgsoni	Oriental Tree Pipit
		Indian Tree Pipit
		Olive Tree Pipit
		Hodgson's Pipit★
	leucophrys	Plain-backed Pipit
		Dark Plain-backed Pipit
	pallidiventris	Long-legged Pipit
		Long-clawed Pipit
	roseatus	Hodgson's Pipit★
		Rosy Pipit
	similis	Long-billed Pipit
		Brown Rock Pipit
	vaalensis	Sandy Plain-backed Pipit
		Buff Plain-backed Pipit

Campephagidae   Cuckoo Shrikes

(Many species alternatively known as Cuckoo Shrikes or Greybirds.)

Coracina	*analis*	Mountain Greybird
		New Caledonian Greybird
	bicolor	Celebes Cuckoo Shrike
		Muna Greybird
	caesia	African Grey Cuckoo Shrike
		Mountain Grey Cuckoo Shrike
	dohertyi	Doherty's Greybird
		Sumba Greybird
	holopolium	Black-bellied Greybird
		Cicada Greybird
	leucopygia	White-rumped Cuckoo Shrike
		Muna Cuckoo Shrike
	melaschistos	Lesser Cuckoo Shrike
		Black-winged Cuckoo Shrike
		Dark Grey Cuckoo Shrike
	novaehollandiae	Large Cuckoo Shrike
		Black-faced Cuckoo Shrike
		White-vented Cuckoo Shrike
	papuensis	Papuan Cuckoo Shrike
		Little Cuckoo Shrike
	polioptera	Grey Cuckoo Shrike
		Indo-Chinese Cuckoo Shrike
	pollens	Able Cuckoo Shrike
		Kei Cuckoo Shrike
	striata	Barred Cuckoo Shrike
		Bar-bellied Cuckoo Shrike
	tenuirostris	Long-billed Greybird
		Cicada Bird
		Jardine's Triller
Lalage	*leucomela*	White-browed Triller
		Varied Triller
Campephaga	*phoenicea*	Red-shouldered Cuckoo Shrike
		Black Cuckoo Shrike★
Pericrocotus	*ethologus*	Flame-coloured Minivet
		Long-tailed Minivet
	lansbergi	Flores Minivet
		Sumbawa Minivet
	solaris	Mountain Minivet
		Grey-chinned Minivet

Campephagidae Cuckoo Shrikes (cont.)

		Yellow-throated Minivet
Tephrodornis	*gularis*	Brown-tailed Wood Shrike
		Large Wood Shrike

Pycnonotidae   Bulbuls

(Some species known alternatively as Bulbuls, Greenbuls or Green Bulbuls.)

Spizixos	*canifrons*	Finch-billed Bulbul
		Crested Finchbill
	semitorques	Collared Finch-billed Bulbul
		Collared Finchbill
Andropadus	*curvirostris*	Sombre Bulbul
		Cassin's Bulbul
	hallae	Hall's Greenbul
		Mrs Hall's Bulbul
	tephrolaemus	Grey-throated Bulbul
		Olive-breasted Mountain Greenbul
Pycnonotus	*aurigaster*	White-eared Bulbul
		Yellow-vented Bulbul*
		Sooty-headed Bulbul
		Golden-vented Bulbul
	barbatus	Common Bulbul
		Black-eyed Bulbul
		White-vented Bulbul
	blanfordi	Blanford's Olive Bulbul
		Blanford's Bulbul
		Streak-eared Bulbul
	erythrophthalmos	Lesser Brown Bulbul
		Spectacled Bulbul
	finlaysoni	Stripe-throated Bulbul
		Streak-throated Bulbul
	flavescens	Pale-faced Bulbul
		Flavescent Bulbul
		Blyth's Bulbul
	jocosus	Red-whiskered Bulbul
		Red-eared Bulbul
		Red-cheeked Bulbul
	leucogrammicus	Striated Bulbul
		Streaked Bulbul
	melanicterus	Black-headed Yellow Bulbul
		Red-throated Bulbul

FAMILY/GENUS	SPECIES/SUBSPECIES	ENGLISH NAMES
		Ruby-throated Bulbul
		Black-crested Bulbul
		Yellow Bulbul
	nieuwenhuisi	Malaysian Wattled Bulbul
		Blue Wattled Bulbul
	nigricans	Black-fronted Bulbul
		Red-eyed Bulbul
	penicillatus	Yellow-eared Bulbul
		Yellow-tufted Bulbul
	plumosus	Olive-brown Bulbul
		Olive-winged Bulbul
	simplex	White-eyed Brown Bulbul
		Cream-vented Bulbul
	sinensis	Chinese Bulbul
		Light-vented Bulbul
	taivanus	Formosan Bulbul
		Styan's Bulbul
	urostictus	Wattled Bulbul
		Yellow Wattled Bulbul
	xanthorrhous	Anderson's Bulbul
		Brown-breasted Bulbul
	zeylanicus	Yellow-crowned Bulbul
		Straw-headed Bulbul
		Straw-coloured Bulbul
Calyptocichla	*serina*	Golden Bulbul
		Serine Greenbul
Baeopogon	*indicator*	White-tailed Bulbul
		Honeyguide Greenbul
Chlorocichla	*flavicollis*	Yellow-throated Leaf-love
		Yellow-throated Bulbul
	flaviventris	Yellow-bellied Greenbul
		Pale Olive Greenbul
	simplex	Simple Bulbul
		Simple Leaf-love
Thescelocichla	*leucopleura*	Swamp Bulbul
		Swamp Palm Bulbul
		White-tailed Greenbul
Phyllastrephus	*flavostriatus*	Yellow-streaked Greenbul
		Yellow-bellied Bulbul
	icterinus	Lesser Icterine Bulbul
		Icterine Bulbul

FAMILY/GENUS	SPECIES/SUBSPECIES	ENGLISH NAMES

Pycnonotidae Bulbuls (cont.)

	lorenzi	Lorenz's Bulbul
		Sassi's Greenbul
	orostruthus	Dappled Mountain-Greenbul
		Dappled Bulbul
	terrestris	Brownbul
		Terrestrial Brownbul
		Terrestrial Bulbul
	xavieri	Greater Icterine Bulbul
		Xavier's Greenbul
Nicator	*chloris*	African Nicator
		Yellow-spotted Nicator
		White-throated Nicator
Criniger	*bres*	Olive White-throated Bulbul
		Grey-cheeked Bearded Bulbul
		Grey-cheeked Bulbul
	calurus	White-bearded Greenbul
		Red-tailed Greenbul
	finschi	Dwarf Bearded Bulbul
		Finsch's Bulbul
	flaveolus	Ashy-fronted Bearded Bulbul
		White-throated Bulbul
	ochraceus	Brown White-throated Bulbul
		Ochraceous Bulbul
	olivaceus	Yellow-throated Olive Bulbul
		Olive Bulbul
	pallidus	Olivaceous Bearded Bulbul
		Puff-throated Bulbul
	phaeocephalus	Crestless White-throated Bulbul
		Crestless Bulbul
		Yellow-bellied Bulbul
Setornis	*criniger*	Hook-billed Bulbul
		Long-billed Bulbul
Hypsipetes	*borbonicus*	Reunion Bulbul
		Olivaceous Bulbul
	charlottae	Crested Olive Bulbul
		Buff-vented Bulbul
		Finsch's Olive Bulbul
		Charlotte's Olive Bulbul
	crassirostris	Seychelles Bulbul
		Thick-billed Bulbul

FAMILY/GENUS	SPECIES/SUBSPECIES	ENGLISH NAMES
	everetti	Yellow-washed Bulbul
		Everett's Bulbul
	flavala	Oriental Brown-eared Bulbul
		Chestnut Bulbul
		Ashy Bulbul
	indicus	Yellow-browed Bulbul
		Yellow-eyebrowed Bulbul
	madagascariensis	Black Bulbul
		Madagascar Bulbul
	malaccensis	Green-backed Bulbul
		Streaked Bulbul
	mcclellandii	McClelland's Bulbul
		McClelland's Rufous-bellied Bulbul
		Mountain Bulbul*
		Mountain Streaked Bulbul
	philippinus	Rufous-breasted Bulbul
		Philippe Rufous Bulbul
	thompsoni	Bingham's Bulbul
		White-headed Bulbul
	virescens	Green-winged Bulbul
		Sumatran Bulbul
	viridescens	Blyth's Olive Bulbul
		Viridescent Bulbul

Irenidae Leafbirds

(All species of genus *Aegithina* alternatively known as Ioras or Leafbirds. All species of genus *Chloropsis* alternatively known as Chloropsis, Leafbirds or Fruit-suckers, and some as Green Bulbuls.)

Chloropsis	*cochinchinensis*	Blue-winged Leafbird
		Golden-mantled Leafbird
		Jerdon's Leafbird
	hardwickii	Orange-bellied Leafbird
		Hardwick's Fruit-sucker
	venusta	Blue-masked Leafbird
		Masked Leafbird
Irena	*cyanogaster*	Philippine Fairy Bluebird
		Black-mantled Fairy Bluebird

FAMILY/GENUS	SPECIES/SUBSPECIES	ENGLISH NAMES

Prionopidae Helmet Shrikes

Prionops *plumata* Long-crested Helmet Shrike
White Helmet Shrike

Laniidae Shrikes

Tchagra *australis* Black-crowned Bush Shrike★
Brown-headed Bush Shrike
minuta Lesser Bush Shrike
Little Blackcap Tchagra
Marsh Tchagra
Black-capped Bush Shrike
senegala Black-headed Bush Shrike
Black-crowned Bush Shrike★
Black-crowned Tchagra
tchagra Levaillant's Bush Shrike
Tchagra Bush Shrike
Laniarius *atrococcineus* Crimson-breasted Shrike
Crimson-breasted Boubou
atroflavus Yellow-breasted Shrike
Yellow-breasted Boubou
barbarus Gonolek
Crimson-breasted Boubou
ferrugineus Southern Boubou
African Boubou
Boubou Shrike
Bell Shrike

(Many species of genus *Malaconotus* alternatively known as Shrikes or Bush Shrikes.)

Malaconotus *bocagei* Bocage's Bush Shrike
Grey Bush Shrike
gladiator Pugnacious Bush Shrike
Green-breasted Shrike
kupeensis Mt Kupe Bush Shrike
Serle's Bush Shrike
multicolor Many-coloured Bush Shrike
Black-fronted Bush Shrike★
quadricolor Gorgeous Bush Shrike★
Four-coloured Shrike
sulfureopectus Orange-breasted Bush Shrike
Sulphur-breasted Bush Shrike
viridis Perrin's Bush Shrike

FAMILY/GENUS	SPECIES/SUBSPECIES	ENGLISH NAMES
		Gorgeous Bush Shrike*
Corvinella	*corvina*	Western Long-tailed Shrike
		Yellow-billed Shrike
	melanoleuca	Eastern Long-tailed Shrike
		Magpie Shrike
Lanius	*collurioides*	Chestnut-backed Shrike
		Burmese Shrike
	excubitor	Northern Shrike
		Great Grey Shrike
	sphenocercus	Long-tailed Grey Shrike
		Chinese Great Grey Shrike
		Chinese Shrike
		Wedge-tailed Shrike
	tephronotus	Tibetan Shrike
		Grey-backed Shrike
	tigrinus	Thick-billed Shrike
		Tiger Shrike
Pityriasis	*gymnocephala*	Bornean Bristlehead
		Bristled Shrike

Vangidae Vanga Shrikes
Calicalicus	*madagascariensis*	Red-tailed Vanga
		Tit Shrike

Ptilogonatidae Waxwings
Bombycilla	*garrulus*	Bohemian Waxwing
		Waxwing
	japonica	Japanese Waxwing
		Eastern Waxwing

Cinclidae Dippers
Cinclus	*cinclus*	Dipper
		White-throated Dipper

Troglodytidae Wrens
Campylo-	*megalopterus*	Grey-barred Wren
rhynchus		Grey Cactus Wren
		Grey Wren
		Great-winged Wren
	zonatus	Band-backed Wren

Troglodytidae Wrens (cont.)

		Banded Wren
Cistothorus	*platensis*	Short-billed Marsh Wren
		Sedge Wren
		Grass Wren
Troglodytes	*troglodytes*	Wren
		Winter Wren

Mimidae   Mockingbirds, Thrashers

Dumetella	*carolinensis*	Grey Catbird
		Common Catbird
Mimus	*saturninus*	Chalk-browed Mockingbird
		Saturnine Mockingbird
Toxostoma	*cinereum*	Grey Thrasher
		Ash-coloured Thrasher
	lecontei	Le Conte's Thrasher
		Desert Thrasher

Prunellidae   Accentors

(Most species alternatively known as Accentors or Dunnocks.)

Prunella	*modularis*	Dunnock
		Hedge Accentor
		Hedge Sparrow

Muscicapidae: s.f. **Turdinae**   Thrushes

(Many species of genus *Cercotrichas* alternatively known as Bush Chats, Scrub Robins or Bush Robins.)

Cercotrichas	*leucophrys*	White-winged Scrub Robin
		White-browed Scrub Robin
		Red-backed Scrub Robin
	leucosticta	Western Bearded Scrub Robin
		Gold Coast Scrub Robin
		Forest Scrub Robin
Pinarornis	*plumosus*	Sooty Rock Chat
		Boulder Chat
Sheppardia	*aequatorialis*	Equatorial Akalat
		Equatorial Redstart
	cyornithopsis	Whiskered Akalat
		Whiskered Redstart

FAMILY/GENUS	SPECIES/SUBSPECIES	ENGLISH NAMES
	gabela	Gabela Akalat
		Gabela Robin
	gunningi	East Coast Akalat
		Gunning's Robin
	sharpei	Sharpe's Akalat
		Sharpe's Robin
Luscinia	*brunnea*	Indian Blue Robin
		Indian Blue Chat
	cyanurus	Orange-flanked Bush Robin
		Red-flanked Bluetail
	luscinia	Thrush Nightingale
		Sprosser
	pectardens	Père David's Orangethroat
		Firethroat
	pectoralis	Himalayan Rubythroat
		White-tailed Rubythroat
	ruficeps	Rufous-headed Robin
		Red-headed Robin
	sibilans	Swinhoe's Red-tailed Robin
		Rufous-tailed Robin

(Many species of genus *Cossypha* alternatively known as Robin Chats, Chats or Robins.)

Cossypha	*albicapilla*	White-crowned Robin Chat
		White-capped Robin Chat
		White-headed Robin Chat
	caffra	Robin Chat
		Cape Robin
	cyanocampter	Blue-shouldered Robin Chat
		Blue-shouldered Redbreast
	heuglini	White-browed Robin Chat
		Heuglin's Robin Chat
		Heuglin's Redbreast
	niveicapilla	Snowy-headed Robin Chat
		White-capped Redbreast
Copsychus	*malabaricus*	White-rumped Shama
		Shama
	saularis	Dyal
		Dyal Bird
		Dyal Thrush
		Magpie Robin
	stricklandii	Black Shama

Muscicapidae: s.f. **Turdinae** Thrushes (cont.)

FAMILY/GENUS	SPECIES/SUBSPECIES	ENGLISH NAMES
		White-crowned Shama
		Strickland's Shama
Hodgsonius	*phoenicuroides*	Hodgson's Shortwing
		White-bellied Redstart
Cercomela	*familiaris*	Red-tailed Chat
		Familiar Chat
	schlegelii	Schlegel's Chat
		Grey-rumped Sickle-winged Chat

(Some species of genus *Saxicola* alternatively known as Stonechats, Bush Chats or Chats.)

Saxicola	*dacotiae*	Canary Island Stonechat
		Meade-Waldo's Chat
Myrmecocichla	*aethiops*	Anteater Chat
		Ant Chat
Oenanthe	*bifasciata*	Buff-streaked Chat
		Buff-streaked Wheatear
	bottae	Red-breasted Wheatear
		Red-breasted Chat
	leucopyga	White-rumped Black Wheatear
		White-crowned Black Wheatear
Saxicoloides	*fulicata*	Indian Robin
		Indian Chat
		Black Robin*
Monticola	*angolensis*	Mottled Rock Thrush
		Angola Rock Thrush
	cinclorhynchus	Blue-headed Rock Thrush
		Blue-capped Rock Thrush
		White-throated Rock Thrush
	saxatilis	Rock Thrush
		Rufous-tailed Rock Thrush
Myiophoneus	*blighi*	Blyth's Whistling Thrush
		Ceylon Whistling Thrush

(All species of genus *Zoothera* alternatively known as Ground Thrushes or Thrushes.)

Zoothera	*andromedae*	Sunda Ground Thrush
		Andromeda Thrush
	citrina	Orange-headed Ground Thrush
		Dama Thrush
	dauma	White's Thrush
		Golden Mountain Thrush

	erythronota	Celebes Ground Thrush
		Lombok Thrush
	interpres	Kuhl's Ground Thrush
		Chestnut-capped Thrush
	marginata	Lesser Long-billed Thrush
		Lesser Brown Thrush
	monticola	Greater Long-billed Thrush
		Large Brown Thrush
	peronii	Peroni's Ground Thrush
		Timor Thrush
	terrestris	Kittlitz's Thrush
		Bonin Thrush

(Most species of genus *Catharus* alternatively known as Nightingale Thrushes or Thrushes.)

Catharus	*ustulatus*	Swainson's Thrush
		Olive-backed Thrush
		Russet-backed Thrush
Turdus	*abyssinicus*	Rufous Thrush
		Jackson's Thrush
		African Mountain Thrush
	cardis	Grey Thrush
		Japanese Thrush
	chrysolaus	Red-bellied Thrush
		Brown-headed Thrush
		Red-billed Thrush
	dissimilis	Black-breasted Thrush
		Grey-backed Thrush
	feae	Fea's Thrush
		Grey-sided Thrush
	fumigatus	Pale-vented Robin
		Cocoa Thrush
	fuscater	Great Thrush
		Brown Thrush
	grayi	Clay-coloured Thrush
		Gray's Thrush
	gurneyi	Orange Ground Thrush
		Gurney's Thrush
	ignobilis	Black-billed Thrush
		Black-billed Robin
	mupinensis	Verreaux's Song Thrush
		Laubmann's Thrush

Muscicapidae: s.f. **Turdinae** Thrushes (cont.)

		Eastern Song Thrush
	naumanni	Dusky Thrush
		Naumann's Thrush
	nigriceps	Slaty Thrush
		Black Robin★
	oberlaenderi	Congo Thrush
		Forest Ground Thrush
	olivaceus	Olive Thrush
		Cape Thrush
	poliocephalus	Mountain Blackbird
		Island Thrush
	rubocanus	Grey-headed Thrush
		Chestnut Thrush
	ruficollis	Red-throated Thrush
		Black-throated Thrush [1]
	serranus	Glossy Black Thrush
		Giant Mountain Robin

Muscicapidae: s.f. **Timaliinae**   Babblers, Wren Tits

Pellorneum	*ruficeps*	Spotted Babbler
		Puff-throated Babbler

(Some species of genus *Trichastoma* alternatively known as Babblers or Jungle Babblers.)

Trichastoma	*cleaveri*	Blackcap Illadopsis
		Blackcap Akalat
	fulvescens	Brown Illadopsis
		Brown Akalat
	rostrata	Blyth's Babbler
		White-chested Babbler
	rufipenne	Pale-breasted Illadopsis
		White-breasted Akalat
	tickelli	Tickell's Babbler
		Buff-breasted Babbler
Ptyrticus	*turdinus*	White-bellied Thrush Babbler
		Spotted Thrush Babbler
Malacopteron	*affine*	Plain Babbler

---

[1] There are two recognised colour forms of this species.

FAMILY/GENUS	SPECIES/SUBSPECIES	ENGLISH NAMES
		Sooty-capped Babbler
	albogulare	White-throated Babbler
		Grey-breasted Babbler
	cinereum	Lesser Red-headed Babbler
		Scaly-crowned Babbler
		Scaly-capped Babbler
	magnirostre	Brown-headed Babbler
		Moustached Babbler
	magnum	Greater Red-headed Babbler
		Red-headed Babbler
		Rufous-crowned Babbler
Pomatorhinus	*horsfieldii*	Horsfield's Scimitar Babbler
		Indian Scimitar Babbler
	montanus	Chestnut-backed Scimitar Babbler
		Yellow-billed Scimitar Babbler
	ruficollis	Rufous-necked Scimitar Babbler
		Streak-breasted Scimitar Babbler
	schisticeps	Slaty-headed Scimitar Babbler
		White-browed Scimitar Babbler
Jabouilleia	*danjoui*	Danjou's Babbler
		Short-tailed Scimitar Babbler
Rimator	*malacoptilus*	Long-billed Wren Babbler
		Long-billed Scimitar Babbler
Ptilocichla	*falcata*	Falcated Ground Babbler
		Falcated Wren Babbler
Napothera	*brevicaudata*	Short-tailed Wren Babbler
		Streaked Wren Babbler
	epilepidota	Small Wren Babbler
		Eye-browed Wren Babbler
	macrodactyla	Large-footed Wren Babbler
		Large Wren Babbler
	marmoratus	Muller's Wren Babbler
		Marbled Wren Babbler
	rabori	Rabor's Wren Babbler
		Luzon Wren Babbler
Pnoepyga	*albiventer*	Greater Scaly Wren Babbler
		Scaly-breasted Wren Babbler
	pusilla	Lesser Scaly Wren Babbler
		Pygmy Wren Babbler
Spelaeornis	*caudatus*	Tailed Wren Babbler
		Rufous-throated Wren Babbler

FAMILY/GENUS	SPECIES/SUBSPECIES	ENGLISH NAMES

Muscicapidae: s.f. **Timaliinae** Babblers, Wren Tits (cont.)

	chocolatinus	Streaked Long-tailed Wren Babbler
		Long-tailed Wren Babbler★
	longicaudatus	Long-tailed Wren Babbler★
		Tawny-breasted Wren Babbler
Neomixis	*tenella*	Northern Jery
		Common Jery
Stachyris	*ambigua*	Equivocal Babbler
		Buff-chested Babbler
		Harington's Babbler
	capitalis	Rufous-crowned Tree Babbler
		Philippine Tree Babbler
	chrysaea	Golden-headed Babbler
		Golden Babbler
	erythroptera	Red-winged Babbler
		Chestnut-winged Babbler
	herberti	Laos Dusky Tree Babbler
		Sooty Babbler
		Herbert's Babbler
	leucotis	White-eared Tree Babbler
		White-necked Babbler
	maculata	Red-rumped Tree Babbler
		Chestnut-rumped Babbler
	nigriceps	Black-throated Babbler★
		Grey-throated Babbler
	nigricollis	Black-necked Tree Babbler
		Black-throated Babbler★
	nigrorum	Black-crowned Tree Babbler
		Negros Tree Babbler
	plateni	Pygmy Tree Babbler
		Platen's Babbler
	pyrrhops	Red-billed Babbler
		Black-chinned Babbler
	ruficeps	Red-headed Tree Babbler
		Rufous-capped Babbler
		Rufous-fronted Babbler
	speciosa	Rough-templed Tree Babbler
		Tweeddale's Babbler
	striolata	Spotted Tree Babbler
		Spot-necked Babbler
Dumetia	*hyperythra*	Rufous-bellied Babbler

FAMILY/GENUS	SPECIES/SUBSPECIES	ENGLISH NAMES
		Tawny-bellied Babbler
Macronous	*flavicollis*	Yellow-collared Tit Babbler
		Grey-faced Tit Babbler★
	gularis	Striped Tit Babbler
		Yellow-breasted Tit Babbler
	kelleyi	Grey-faced Tit Babbler★
		Kelley's Tit Babbler
Timalia	*pileata*	Red-capped Babbler
		Chestnut-capped Babbler
Chrysomma	*sinensis*	Yellow-eyed Babbler
		Golden-eyed Babbler
Turdoides	*affinis*	Indian White-headed Babbler
		Yellow-billed Babbler
	aylmeri	Scaly Chatterer
		Aylmer's Babbler
	bicolor	Pied Babbler★
		Bicoloured Babbler
	earlei	Striated Babbler
		Earle's Babbler
	fulvus	Fulvous Babbler
		Fulvous Chatterer
	hypoleucus	Northern Pied Babbler
		Pied Babbler★
	malcolmi	Large Grey Babbler
		Great Grey Babbler
		Malcolm's Babbler
	melanops	Black-lored Babbler
		Black-faced Babbler
	reinwardtii	Western Dusky Babbler
		Blackcap Babbler
	squamiceps	Arabian Brown Babbler
		Arabian Babbler
	striatus	Jungle Babbler
		Striated Babbler
Babax	*lanceolatus*	Chinese Babax
		Common Babax
Garrulax	*caerulatus*	Grey-sided Laughing Thrush
		Fukien Rufous Jay Thrush
	canorus	Hwa-mei
		Hwa-mei Laughing Thrush
		Hoami

Muscicapidae: s.f. **Timaliinae** Babblers, Wren Tits (cont.)

		Melodious Jay Thrush
		Spectacled Jay Thrush
		Brown Laughing Thrush
	chinensis	Black-throated Laughing Thrush
		Chinese Laughing Thrush
	cineraceus	Ashy Laughing Thrush
		Moustached Laughing Thrush
	delesserti	Wynaad Laughing Thrush
		Rufous-vented Laughing Thrush
	davidi	Père David's Laughing Thrush
		Pekin Hill Babbler
	erythrocephalus	Red-headed Laughing Thrush
		Chestnut-crowned Laughing Thrush
	galbanus	Austen's Laughing Thrush
		Yellow-throated Laughing Thrush
	henrici	Prince d'Orlean's Laughing Thrush
		Prince Henry's Laughing Thrush
	maesi	Maes's Laughing Thrush
		Grey Laughing Thrush
	milleti	Millet's Laughing Thrush
		Black-hooded Laughing Thrush
	mitratus	Chestnut-capped Laughing Thrush
		Red-capped Laughing Thrush
		Capped Laughing Thrush
	moniliger	Lesser Necklaced Laughing Thrush
		Necklaced Laughing Thrush
	pectoralis	Greater Necklaced Laughing Thrush
		Gorgeted Laughing Thrush
	perspicillatus	Spectacled Laughing Thrush
		Masked Laughing Thrush
	sannio	White-browed Laughing Thrush
		White-cheeked Laughing Thrush
	strepitans	Tickell's Laughing Thrush
		White-necked Laughing Thrush
	subunicolor	Plain-coloured Laughing Thrush
		Scaly Laughing Thrush
	virgatus	Streaked Laughing Thrush★
		Striped Laughing Thrush
Liocichla	*phoenicea*	Crimson-winged Liocichla
		Red-faced Liocichla

FAMILY/GENUS	SPECIES/SUBSPECIES	ENGLISH NAMES
Leiothrix	*lutea*	Pekin Robin
		Pekin Nightingale
		Red-billed Leiothrix
Pteruthius	*flaviscapis*	Red-winged Shrike Babbler
		White-browed Shrike Babbler
		Black-crowned Shrike Babbler
		Greater Shrike Babbler
	melanotis	Chestnut-throated Shrike Babbler
		Black-eared Shrike Babbler
	rufiventer	Rufous-bellied Shrike Babbler
		Black-headed Shrike Babbler
Gampsorhynchus	*rufulus*	White-headed Shrike Babbler
		Black-headed Shrike Babbler
Actinodura	*egertoni*	Spectacled Barwing★
		Rusty-footed Barwing
	ramsayi	Ramsay's Barwing
		Spectacled Barwing★
	souliei	Soule's Barwing
		Streaked Barwing
	waldeni	Austen's Barwing
		Walden's Barwing
		Streak-throated Barwing
Minla	*cyanouroptera*	Blue-winged Siva
		Blue-winged Minla
	ignotincta	Fire-tailed Minla
		Red-tailed Minla
	strigula	Bar-throated Minla
		Chestnut-tailed Minla
		Bar-throated Siva

(The genus *Alcippe* consists of Tit Babblers, Quaker Babblers and Nun Babblers, all are alternatively known as Fulvettas.)

Alcippe	*abyssinica*	African Hill Babbler
		Mountain Babbler
	brunnea	Gould's Tit Babbler
		Brown-capped Fulvetta
	castaneceps	Chestnut-headed Tit Babbler
		Rufous-winged Fulvetta
	cinerea	Yellow-throated Tit Babbler
		Dusky Fulvetta
	cinereiceps	Grey-headed Tit Babbler

Muscicapidae: s.f. **Timaliinae** Babblers, Wren Tits (cont.)

		Brown-headed Fulvetta
		Streak-throated Fulvetta
	morrisonia	Grey-headed Quaker Babbler
		Grey-cheeked Fulvetta
	nipalensis	White-eyed Quaker Babbler
		Nepal Quaker Babbler
	poioicephala	Quaker Babbler
		Brown-cheeked Fulvetta
	ruficapilla	Verreaux's Rufous-headed Tit Babbler
		Spectacled Fulvetta
	rufogularis	Red-throated Tit Babbler
		Rufous-throated Fulvetta
	striaticollis	Mountain Tit Babbler
		Striped Fulvetta
Lioptilus	*gilberti*	White-throated Mountain Babbler
		Gilbert's Babbler
	nigricapillus	Blackcap Babbler
		Bush Blackcap
	rufocinctus	Rufous-collared Mountain Babbler
		Red-collared Flycatcher
Phyllanthus	*atripennis*	Capuchin Babbler
		Black-winged Babbler
Heterophasia	*annectens*	Chestnut-backed Sibia
		Rufous-backed Sibia
	capistrata	Black-headed Sibia*
		Black-capped Sibia
		Rufous Sibia
	melanoleuca	Tickell's Sibia
		Black-headed Sibia*
Picathartes	*gymnocephalus*	Guinea Bare-headed Rock Fowl
		White-necked Rock Fowl
		White-necked Bald Crow
		White-necked Guinea Fowl
		Yellow-headed Picathartes
	oreas	Cameroon Bare-headed Rock Fowl
		Grey-necked Rock Fowl
		Grey-necked Bald Crow
		Red-headed Picathartes

(All species of genus *Yuhina* alternatively known as Yuhinas, Ixulas and Crested Babblers.)

Yuhina	*bakeri*	Baker's Chestnut-headed Yuhina
		White-naped Yuhina
		Blyth's Yuhina
	castaniceps	Chestnut-headed Yuhina
		Striated Yuhina
		White-browed Yuhina
	diademata	White-collared Yuhina
		Diademed Yuhina
	flavicollis	Yellow-naped Yuhina
		Whiskered Yuhina
		Yellow-collared Ixulus
	gularis	Stripe-throated Yuhina
		Striped Yuhina
	nigrimenta	Black-chinned Yuhina
		Black-chinned Flower-pecker
		Black-crested Babbler
	occipitalis	Rufous-vented Yuhina
		Slaty-headed Yuhina
Oxylabes	*madagascariensis*	Foditany
		Oxylabes

Muscicapidae: s.f. Paradoxornithinae   Parrotbills

Panurus	*biarmicus*	Bearded Reedling
		Bearded Tit
Paradoxornis	*alphonsianus*	Ashy-throated Parrotbill
		Verreaux's Parrotbill
	atrosuperciliaris	Black-browed Parrotbill
		Lesser Red-headed Parrotbill
		Lesser Rufous-headed Parrotbill
	davidianus	Short-tailed Parrotbill
		David's Parrotbill
	flavirostris	Gould's Parrotbill
		Black-breasted Parrotbill
	fulvifrons	Fulvous-fronted Parrotbill
		Fulvous Parrotbill
	guttaticollis	Spot-breasted Parrotbill
		Rufous-headed Parrotbill
	heudei	Yangtze Crowtit

Muscicapidae: s.f. **Paradoxornithinae** Parrotbills (cont.)

		Heude's Parrotbill
		Chinese Parrotbill
	nipalensis	Ashy-eared Parrotbill
		Orange Parrotbill
		Black-throated Parrotbill
		Nepal Parrotbill
	przewalskii	Przevalski's Parrotbill
		Grey-crowned Parrotbill
	ricketti	Yunnan Parrotbill
		Rickett's Parrotbill
	ruficeps	Greater Red-headed Parrotbill
		Greater Rufous-headed Parrotbill
	webbianus	Vinous-throated Parrotbill
		Webb's Parrotbill
	zappeyi	Zappey's Parrotbill
		Dusky Parrotbill

Muscicapidae: s.f. **Sylviinae**   Old World Warblers

Cettia	*acanthizoides*	Verreaux's Bush Warbler
		Yellowish-bellied Bush Warbler
	brunnifrons	Rufous-capped Bush Warbler
		Grey-sided Bush Warbler
	fortipes	Strong-footed Bush Warbler
		Brownish-flanked Bush Warbler
	major	Large Bush Warbler
		Chestnut-crowned Bush Warbler
	squamciceps	Short-tailed Bush Warbler
		Stub-tailed Bush Warbler
		Scaly-headed Bush Warbler
Bradypterus	*accentor*	Kinabalu Scrub Warbler
		Friendly Warbler
	alfredi	Bamboo Warbler
		Newton's Scrub Warbler
	baboecala	African Sedge Warbler
		Swamp Warbler
		Little Rush Warbler
	castaneus	East Indies Bush Warbler
		Chestnut Grass Warbler
	cinnamomeus	Cinnamon Bracken Warbler
		Long-tailed Forest Scrub Warbler

FAMILY/GENUS	SPECIES/SUBSPECIES	ENGLISH NAMES
	palliseri	Palliser's Warbler
		Ceylon Bush Warbler
	seebohmi	Mountain Scrub Warbler
		Mountain Bush Warbler
		Russet Bush Warbler
Megalurus	*gramineus*	Little Grass Warbler
		Little Grassbird
	timoriensis	Rufous-capped Grass Warbler
		Tawny Grassbird
Locustella	*fasciolata*	Gray's Grasshopper Warbler
		Large Grasshopper Warbler
Acrocephalus	*gracilirostris*	Cape Reed Warbler
		Lesser Swamp Warbler
	stentoreus	Southern Great Reed Warbler
		Clamorous Reed Warbler
Chloropeta	*gracilirostris*	Thin-billed Flycatcher
		Yellow Swamp Warbler
	natalensis	Yellow Flycatcher
		African Yellow Warbler
	similis	Mountain Yellow Flycatcher
		Yellow Mountain Warbler
Sylvia	*leucomelana*	Red Sea Warbler
		Arabian Warbler

(The genus *Phylloscopus* consists of Willow Warblers, Leaf Warblers and Woodland Warblers but many are sometimes shown as just Warblers.)

Phylloscopus	*laurae*	Mrs Boulton's Woodland Warbler
		Laura's Warbler
Seicercus	*burkii*	Yellow-eyed Flycatcher Warbler
		Black-browed Flycatcher Warbler

(The genus *Prinia* consists of Wren Warblers, Grass Warblers and Long-tailed Warblers and all are alternatively known as Prinias.)

Prinia	*atrogularis*	Black-throated Prinia
		Hill Prinia
	cinereocapilla	Hodgson's Long-tailed Warbler
		Grey-crowned Prinia
	clamans	Cricket Warbler
		Scaly Prinia
	criniger	Hill Warbler
		Brown Hill Warbler
		Striated Prinia
	flavicans	Black-chested Prinia

Muscicapidae: s.f. **Sylviinae** Old World Warblers (cont.)

		Black-cheeked Prinia
	gracilis	Graceful Prinia
		Graceful Warbler
	hodgsoni	Franklin's Wren Warbler
		Ashy-grey Prinia
		Grey-breasted Prinia
	inornata	Greater Brown Wren Warbler
		Plain Prinia
	rufescens	Dark-crowned Wren Warbler
		Rufescent Prinia
	subflava	Tawny Prinia
		Tawny-flanked Prinia
		Indian Prinia
Scotocerca	*inquieta*	Streaked Scrub Warbler
		Striated Scrub Warbler
Cisticola	*aberrans*	Rock-loving Cisticola
		Rock Cisticola
		Lazy Cisticola
	ayresii	Ayres's Cloud Cisticola
		Wing-snapping Cisticola
		Crackling Cloud Cisticola
	brachyptera	Short-winged Cisticola
		Siffling Cisticola
	brunnescens	Pale-crowned Cloud Cisticola
		Silent Cloud Cisticola
		Pectoral Patch Cisticola
	dambo	Cloud-scraper Cisticola
		Black-tailed Cisticola
	exilis	Golden-headed Cisticola
		Bright-capped Cisticola
	fulvicapilla	Piping Cisticola
		Tawny-headed Grass Warbler
		Short-tailed Neddicky
	galactotes	Winding Cisticola
		Greater Black-headed Cisticola
	hunteri	Hunter's Cisticola
		Mountain Cisticola
	juncidis	Zitting Cisticola
		Streaked Cisticola
		Streaked Fan-tailed Warbler

FAMILY/GENUS	SPECIES/SUBSPECIES	ENGLISH NAMES
		Fan-tailed Warbler
		Fan-tailed Cisticola
	melanura	Angola Slender-tailed Cisticola
		Black-tailed Cisticola
	rufa	Rufous Grass Warbler
		Rufous Cisticola
	rufilata	Tinkling Cisticola
		Grey Cisticola
	textrix	Cloud Cisticola
		Spotted Cloud Cisticola
	tinniens	Le Vaillant's Cisticola
		Lesser Black-headed Cisticola
Apalis	*cinerea*	Grey Apalis
		Brown-headed Apalis
	flavida	Yellow-breasted Apalis
		Black-breasted Apalis
	pulchella	Acacia Warbler
		Buff-bellied Apalis
Camaroptera	*brachyura*	Broad-tailed Camaroptera
		Bleating Bush Warbler
	simplex	Grey Wren Warbler
		Plain Bush Warbler
	stierlingi	Stierling's Barred Wren Warbler
		Eastern Barred Bush Warbler
Eremomela	*atricollis*	Black-necked Eremomela
		Black-collared Eremomela
	icteropygialis	Yellow-backed Eremomela
		Yellow-bellied Eremomela

Muscicapidae: s.f. **Malurinae**   Wren Warblers

(The genus *Malurus* consists of Wren Warblers and Blue Wrens and many are often shown just as Wrens.)

Malurus	*coronatus*	Purple-crowned Wren Warbler
		Lilac-crowned Wren
	leucopterus	Blue and White Wren Warbler
		White-winged Wren
Amytornis	*textilis*	Western Grass Wren
		Thick-billed Grass Wren

FAMILY/GENUS	SPECIES/SUBSPECIES	ENGLISH NAMES

Muscicapidae: s.f. **Acanthizinae** — Australasian Warblers

Aphelocephala	*leucopsis*	Common Whiteface
		Southern Whiteface
Acanthiza	*iredalei*	Slender Thornbill
		Samphire Thornbill
	nana	Little Thornbill
		Yellow Thornbill
	robustirostris	Robust Thornbill
		Slate-backed Thornbill
Hylacola	*cauta*	Shy Ground Wren
		Shy Heath Wren
	pyrrhopygia	Chestnut-tailed Ground Wren
		Chestnut-tailed Heath Wren

(All species of genus *Gerygone* alternatively known as Warblers or Gerygone Warblers.)

Gerygone	*chloronota*	Grey-headed Gerygone Warbler
		Green-backed Warbler
	fusca	Western Gerygone Warbler
		White-tailed Warbler
	levigaster	Buff-breasted Gerygone Warbler
		Mangrove Warbler
	magnirostris	Swamp Gerygone Warbler
		Large-billed Warbler
	palpebrosa	Black-headed Gerygone Warbler
		Black-throated Warbler

(Many species of genus *Sericornis* alternatively known as Scrub Wrens or Sericornis.)

Sericornis	*beccarii*	Beccari's Sericornis
		Little Scrub Wren

Muscicapidae: s.f. **Muscicapinae** — Old World Flycatchers

Bradornis	*pallidus*	Pale Flycatcher
		Mouse-coloured Flycatcher
Rhinomyias	*brunneata*	White-gorgeted Jungle Flycatcher
		Brown-chested Flycatcher
	olivacea	Olive-backed Jungle Flycatcher
		Fulvous-chested Flycatcher
	umbratilis	White-throated Jungle Flycatcher

		Grey-chested Flycatcher
Ficedula	*cyanomelana*	Blue and White Flycatcher
		Japanese Blue Flycatcher
	hyperythra	White-fronted Blue Flycatcher
		Snowy-browed Flycatcher
		Rufous-breasted Blue Flycatcher
		Dull Flycatcher
	mugimaki	Black and Orange Flycatcher*
		Mugimaki Flycatcher
	narcissina	Black and Yellow Flycatcher
		Narcissus Flycatcher
	nigrorufa	Black and Rufous Flycatcher
		Black and Orange Flycatcher*
	parva	Red-breasted Flycatcher
		Red-throated Flycatcher
	solitaria	Rufous-browed Flycatcher
		White-throated Flycatcher
		Solitary Flycatcher
	superciliaris	White-browed Blue Flycatcher
		Ultramarine Flycatcher
	zanthopygia	Yellow-rumped Flycatcher
		Korean Flycatcher
		Tricoloured Flycatcher

(All species of genus *Niltava* are alternatively known as Niltavas, Flycatchers or Blue Flycatchers.)

Niltava	*grandis*	Large Niltava
		Greater Niltava
	macgrigoriae	Small Niltava
		Lesser Niltava
	poliogenys	Brook's Niltava
		Pale-chinned Flycatcher
	sundara	Rufous-bellied Niltava
		Red-bellied Niltava
Muscicapa	*griseisticta*	Grey-spotted Flycatcher
		Grey-streaked Flycatcher
	sibirica	Sooty Flycatcher
		Dark-sided Flycatcher
	sordida	Dusky Blue Flycatcher
		Sordid Flycatcher

Muscicapidae: s.f. **Muscicapinae** Old World Flycatchers (cont.)
(All species of genus *Microeca* alternatively known as Microecas or
Flycatchers.)

Microeca	*griseoceps*	Yellow-footed Microeca
		Yellow Flycatcher

(All species of genus *Petroica* alternatively known as Robin Flycatchers or
Robins.)

Petroica	*traversi*	Chatham Island Robin Flycatcher
		Black Robin*

Muscicapidae: s.f. **Rhipidurinae**   Fantail Flycatchers

Rhipidura	*albicollis*	White-throated Fantail Flycatcher
		White-spotted Fantail
	cyaniceps	Blue-headed Fantail
		Rufous-bellied Fantail
	javanica	Pied Fantail Flycatcher
		Malaysian Fantail
	leucophrys	Willie Wagtail
		Black and White Fantail
	perlata	Spotted Fantail Flycatcher
		Perlated Fantail
	rufidorsa	Grey-breasted Rufous Fantail
		Red-backed Fantail
	rufifrons	Rufous-fronted Fantail
		Rufous Fantail
	rufiventris	White-throated Fantail
		Red-vented Fantail
		Northern Fantail

Muscicapidae: s.f. **Monarchinae**   Monarch Flycatchers
(All species of the genus *Batis* alternatively known as Batis, Puff-back
Flycatcher or Puffback.)

Batis	*margaritae*	Boulton's Puff-back Flycatcher
		Margaret's Batis
	molitor	Chin-spot Puff-back Flycatcher
		White-flanked Flycatcher
Trochocercus	*cyanomelas*	Cape Crested Flycatcher
		Blue-mantled Crested Flycatcher
	nigromitratus	Black-crowned Crested Flycatcher
		Black Mitred Flycatcher

		Dusky Crested Flycatcher
Terpsiphone	*atrocaudata*	Black Paradise Flycatcher
		Japanese Paradise Flycatcher
	rufiventer	Red-bellied Paradise Flycatcher
		Black-headed Paradise Flycatcher

(All species of genus *Monarcha* alternatively known as Monarch Flycatchers or Flycatchers.)

Monarcha	*cinerascens*	Islet Monarch
		Ashy Monarch
	frater	Black-winged Monarch Flycatcher
		Pearly Flycatcher
	infelix	Admiralty Island Monarch Flycatcher
		Unhappy Monarch
	leucurus	Kei Monarch Flycatcher
		White-tailed Monarch
	mundus	Tenimber Monarch Flycatcher
		Mundane Monarch
	pileatus	Tufted Monarch Flycatcher
		Pileated Monarch
	sacerdotum	Mee's Monarch Flycatcher
		Priestly Monarch
	verticalis	New Britain Pied Monarch
		Duke of York's Monarch

Muscicapidae: s.f. **Pachycephalinae**   Whistlers, Shrike Thrushes

Pachycephala	*rufogularis*	Red-throated Whistler
		Red-lored Whistler
Colluricincla	*woodwardi*	Brown-breasted Shrike Thrush
		Sandstone Shrike Thrush
Turnagra	*capensis*	Piopio
		New Zealand Thrush

Aegithalidae   Long-Tailed Tits

Aegithalos	*concinnus*	Red-headed Long-tailed Tit
		Black-throated Tit
	iouschistos	Blyth's Long-tailed Tit
		Black-browed Tit

FAMILY/GENUS	SPECIES/SUBSPECIES	ENGLISH NAMES

Remizidae Penduline Tits

Remiz	*caroli*	African Penduline Tit
		Grey Penduline Tit
	parvulus	Yellow Penduline Tit
		West African Penduline Tit

Paridae Tits, Titmice, Chickadees

Parus	*afer*	Grey Tit*
		Acacia Grey Tit
	albiventris	White-breasted Tit
		White-bellied Tit
	cinctus	Siberian Tit
		Grey-headed Chickadee
	davidi	Père David's Tit
		Red-bellied Tit*
	dichrous	Brown Crested Tit
		Grey Crested Tit
	griseiventris	Northern Grey Tit
		Miombo Grey Tit
	hudsonicus	Boreal Chickadee
		Brown-capped Chickadee
		Hudsonian Chickadee
		Columbian Chickadee
		Acadian Chickadee
	leucomelas	Black Tit
		White-shouldered Black Tit
		White-winged Black Tit*
	major	Great Tit
		Grey Tit [1]*
		Indian Grey Tit
	nuchalis	White-winged Black Tit*
		White-naped Tit
	rubidiventris	Black-crested Tit
		Rufous-vented Tit
		Red-bellied Tit*
	rufiventris	Cinnamon-breasted Tit
		Rufous-bellied Tit
	sclateri	Mexican Chickadee
		Grey-sided Chickadee

[1] Name given to several races on Indian subcontinent.

	varius	Varied Tit
		Japanese Tit
		Japanese Tumbler
	xanthogenys	Black-spotted Yellow Tit
		Yellow-cheeked Tit

Sittidae   Nuthatches

Sitta	*castanea*	Chestnut-breasted Nuthatch
		Chestnut-bellied Nuthatch
		Dwarf Nuthatch
	himalayensis	White-tailed Nuthatch
		Himalayan Nuthatch
	neumayer	Neumayer's Rock Nuthatch
		Neumayer's Nuthatch
		Lesser Rock Nuthatch
	tephronota	Rock Nuthatch
		Greater Rock Nuthatch
		Eastern Rock Nuthatch
	villosa	Black-headed Nuthatch
		Chinese Nuthatch

Dicaeidae   Flower-peckers

Dicaeum	*aeruginosum*	Fairy Flower-pecker
		Striped Flower-pecker
	annae	Anna's Flower-pecker
		Flores Flower-pecker
	anthonyi	Yellow-crowned Flower-pecker
		Anthony's Flower-pecker
	aureolimbatum	Golden-edged Flower-pecker
		Minahassa Flower-pecker
	australe	Philippine Flower-pecker
		Austral Flower-pecker
	cruentatum	Scarlet-backed Flower-pecker
		Red-backed Flower-pecker
	erythrorhynchos	Tickell's Flower-pecker
		Pale-billed Flower-pecker
	erythrothorax	Reddish Flower-pecker
		Buru Flower-pecker
	eximium	Bismarck Flower-pecker
		Beautiful Flower-pecker

Dicaeidae Flower-Peckers (cont.)

	hirundinaceum	Mistletoe Flower-pecker
		Australian Flower-pecker
	igniferum	Rusty Flower-pecker
		Black-banded Flower-pecker
	ignipectus	Fire-breasted Flower-pecker
		Red-breasted Flower-pecker
		Buff-bellied Flower-pecker
	maugei	Mauge's Flowerpecker
		Blue-cheeked Flowerpecker
	pectorale	Olive-crowned Flowerpecker
		Papuan Flowerpecker

(All species of genus *Pardalotus* alternatively known as Pardolates or Diamond Birds.)

Pardalotus	*ornatus*	Red-tipped Pardalote
		Eastern Striated Pardalote

Nectariniidae   Sunbirds

Anthreptes	*anchietae*	Anchieta's Sunbird
		Red and Blue Sunbird
	gabonicus	Mouse-brown Sunbird
		Brown Sunbird
	longuemarei	Violet-backed Sunbird
		Western Violet-backed Sunbird
	malacensis	Brown-throated Sunbird
		Plain-throated Sunbird
	neglectus	Uluguru Violet-backed Sunbird
		Uluguru Sunbird
	orientalis	Eastern Violet-backed Sunbird
		Kenyan Violet-backed Sunbird
	platura	Pygmy Sunbird
		Pygmy Long-tailed Sunbird
	pujoli	Pujoli Sunbird
		Berlioz's Sunbird
	rhodolaema	Rufous-throated Sunbird
		Red-throated Sunbird
Hypogramma	*hypogrammica*	Blue-naped Sunbird
		Purple-naped Sunbird
Nectarinia	*amethystina*	Amethyst Sunbird
		Black Sunbird
	bannermani	Bannerman's Sunbird

	Blue-headed Sunbird★
chalcostetha	Macklot's Sunbird
	Copper-throated Sunbird
chalybea	Southern Double-collared Sunbird
	Lesser Double-collared Sunbird
congensis	Black-bellied Sunbird
	Congo Sunbird
famosa	Malachite Sunbird
	Yellow-tufted Malachite Sunbird
hartlaubi	Principe Island Sunbird
	Hartlaub's Sunbird
johannae	Scarlet-tufted Malachite Sunbird★
	Johanna's Sunbird
	Madame Johanna Verreaux's Sunbird
johnstoni	Johnston's Malachite Sunbird
	Scarlet-tufted Malachite Sunbird★
jugularis	Yellow-breasted Sunbird
	Olive-backed Sunbird★
lotenia	Loten's Sunbird
	Maroon-breasted Sunbird
	Long-billed Sunbird
newtonii	Sao Thomé Yellow-breasted Sunbird
	Newton's Sunbird
notata	Pemba Violet-breasted Sunbird
	Madagascar Green Sunbird
oritis	Green-headed Sunbird
	Cameroon Sunbird
osea	Orange-tufted Sunbird★
	Northern Orange-tufted Sunbird
	Palestine Sunbird
oustaleti	Angola White-bellied Sunbird
	Oustalet's White-bellied Sunbird
	Angola Sunbird
pembae	Violet-breasted Sunbird
	Pemba Sunbird
pulchella	Beautiful Sunbird
	Beautiful Long-tailed Sunbird
senegalensis	Scarlet-chested Sunbird
	Scarlet-breasted Sunbird
sperata	Van Hesselt's Sunbird
	Purple-throated Sunbird

Nectariniidae Sunbirds (cont.)

	talatala	White-bellied Sunbird
		White-breasted Sunbird
	ursulae	Ursula's Sunbird
		Fernando Po Sunbird
	venusta	Variable Sunbird
		Yellow-bellied Sunbird
	verticalis	Olive-backed Sunbird★
		Green-headed Sunbird
Aethopyga	*duyvenbodei*	Sanghir Sunbird
		Duyvenbode's Sunbird
	gouldiae	Mrs Gould's Sunbird
		Gould's Sunbird
	pulcherrima	Mountain Sunbird
		Loveliest Sunbird
	saturata	Black-breasted Sunbird
		Black-throated Sunbird
	siparaja	Yellow-backed Sunbird
		Crimson Sunbird
Arachnothera	*chrysogenys*	Lesser Yellow-eared Spider-hunter
		Yellow-eared Spider-hunter
	clarae	Bare-faced Spider-hunter
		Naked-faced Spider-hunter
	flavigaster	Greater Yellow-eared Spider-hunter
		Spectacled Spider-hunter

Zosteropidae White-eyes

(All species alternatively known as White-eyes or Zosterops.)

Zosterops	*albogularis*	Norfolk Island White-eye
		White-chested White-eye
		White-breasted Silver-eye
	atrifrons	White-fronted White-eye
		Black-fronted White-eye
	flava	Javan White-eye
		Yellow White-eye★
	flavifrons	Yellow White-eye★
		Yellow-fronted White-eye
	lateralis	Grey-breasted Silver-eye
		Grey-breasted White-eye
		Grey-backed White-eye
		New Zealand Zosterops

	lutea	Mangrove White-eye
		Yellow Silver-eye
		Yellow White-eye★
	mayottensis	Chestnut-flanked White-eye
		Chestnut-sided White-eye
	metcalfei	Yellow-throated White-eye
		Metcalf's White-eye
	modesta	Seychelles Grey White-eye
		Seychelles Brown White-eye
	mouroniensis	Mount Karthala Green White-eye
		Grand Comoro White-eye
	palpebrosa	Oriental White-eye
		Indian White-eye
	virens	Green White-eye
		Natal Zosterops
	wallacei	Wallace's White-eye
		Yellow-spectacled White-eye
Meliphagidae	Honey-eaters	
Glycichaera	*fallax*	White-eyed Honey-eater
		Green-backed Honey-eater
Lichmera	*cockerelli*	Cockerell's Honey-eater
		White-streaked Honey-eater
Certhionyx	*niger*	Dark Honey-eater
		Black Honey-eater
Meliphaga	*cassidix*	Helmeted Honey-eater
		Sub-crested Honey-eater
	chrysops	Yellow-faced Honey-eater
		Black-cheeked Honey-eater
	gracilis	Slender-billed Meliphaga
		Graceful Honey-eater
Philemon	*buceroides*	Noisy Friarbird★
		Sandstone Friarbird
	citreogularis	Yellow-throated Friarbird
		Little Friarbird
	corniculutus	Bald Friarbird
		Noisy Friarbird★
	novaeguineae	Leatherhead
		Helmeted Friarbird
		New Guinea Friarbird
Manorina	*melanotis*	Dusky Miner

Meliphagidae Honey-eaters (cont.)

		Black-eared Miner
Prosthemadera	*novaeseelandiae*	Tui
		Parson Bird

Emberizidae: s.f. Emberizinae   Buntings, American Sparrows

Melopus	*lathami*	Crested Bunting
		Crested Black Bunting
Emberiza	*aureola*	Yellow-breasted Bunting
		Golden Bunting
	cabanisi	Cabanis's Bunting
		Cabanis's Yellow Bunting
	calandra	Corn Bunting
		Common Bunting★
	capensis	Southern Rock Bunting
		Cape Rock Bunting
		Cape Bunting
	cia	Rock Bunting★
		Mountain Bunting
	cineracea	Ashy-headed Bunting
		Cinerous Bunting
	cioides	Long-tailed Bunting
		Meadow Bunting
	citrinella	Yellowhammer
		Yellow Bunting
		Common Bunting★
	elegans	Yellow-throated Bunting
		Elegant Bunting
		Yellow-browed Bunting★
	flaviventris	Golden-breasted Bunting
		Red-backed Yellow Bunting
	fucata	Grey-hooded Bunting
		Grey-headed Bunting
		Chestnut-headed Bunting
	impetuana	Pale Rock Bunting
		Lark-like Bunting
		Lark Bunting
	pusilla	Little Bunting
		Tiny Bunting
	rutila	Chestnut Bunting
		Rufous Bunting

FAMILY/GENUS	SPECIES/SUBSPECIES	ENGLISH NAMES
	spodocephala	Black-faced Bunting
		Grey-headed Bunting
		Masked Bunting
	stewarti	White-capped Bunting
		Chestnut-breasted Bunting★
		Stewart's Bunting
	striolata	Striped Bunting
		House Bunting
	tahapisi	Cinnamon-breasted Rock Bunting
		Cinnamon-breasted Bunting
		Chestnut-breasted Bunting★
		Rock Bunting★
		Seven-striped Bunting
	yessoensis	Far Eastern Reed Bunting
		Japanese Reed Bunting
		Swinhoe's Bunting
Calcarius	*lapponicus*	Lapland Longspur
		Lapland Bunting
Zonotrichia	*capensis*	Rufous-collared Sparrow
		Song Sparrow★
		Andean Sparrow
	leucophrys	White-crowned Sparrow
		White-browed Sparrow
		Song Sparrow★
Junco	*oreganus*	Western Junco
		Oregan Junco
	phaeonotus	Dark-eyed Junco
		Yellow-eyed Junco★
		Red-backed Junco
		Mexican Junco
	vulcani	Yellow-eyed Junco★
		Volcano Junco
Xenospiza	*baileyi*	Sierra Madre Sparrow
		Bailey's Sparrow
Amphispiza	*belli*	Sage Sparrow
		Bell's Sparrow
	bilineata	Black-throated Sparrow
		Desert Sparrow
Aimophila	*ruficauda*	Stripe-headed Sparrow
		Russet-tailed Sparrow
	sumichrasti	Cinnamon-tailed Sparrow

Emberizidae: s.f. **Emberizinae** Buntings, American Sparrows (cont.)

		Sumichrast's Sparrow
Phrygilus	*alaudinus*	Band-tailed Sierra Finch
		Alaudine Finch
		Lark-like Finch
	atriceps	Black-hooded Sierra Finch
		Black-headed Sierra Finch
	fructiceti	Mourning Sierra Finch
		Mourning Finch
		Orchard Finch
		Black Finch
	plebejus	Ash-breasted Sierra Finch
		Lesser Plumbeous Finch
		Grey Finch
	unicolor	Plumbeous Sierra Finch
		Plumbeous Finch
Lophospingus	*griseocristatus*	Grey-crested Finch
		Pygmy Cardinal
Nesospiza	*acunhae*	Tristan Finch
		Tristan Bunting
	wilkinsi	Tristan Grosbeak
		Wilkin's Bunting
		Big-billed Bunting
Poospiza	*melanoleuca*	Black-capped Warbling Finch
		Grey and White Warbling Finch
	nigrorufa	Black and Rufous Warbling Finch
		Chestnut and Black Warbling Finch
	ornata	Cinnamon Warbling Finch
		Pretty Warbling Finch
Sicalis	*citrina*	Stripe-tailed Yellow Finch
		Citrine Finch
		Citrine Grass Finch
	columbiana	Orange-fronted Yellow Finch
		Orange-fronted Finch
		Little Saffron Finch*
		Lesser Saffron Finch
	luteola	Grassland Yellow Finch
		Yellowish Finch
		Yellow Grass Finch
		Yellow-breasted Grass Finch
		Yellow Finch

		Little Saffron Finch★
		Wild Canary
Volatinia	*jacarina*	Blue-black Grassquit
		Blue-black Seedeater
		Jacarini Finch

(Many species of genus *Sporophila* alternatively known as Seedeaters or Finches.)

Sporophila	*americana*	Variable Seedeater
		Tobago Finch
		Black Seedeater
	bouvreuil	Capped Seedeater
		Reddish Finch
	bouvronoides	Black-headed Lined Finch
		Lesson's Seedeater
	caerulescens	Double-collared Seedeater
		Bluish Finch
	castaneiventris	Chestnut-bellied Seedeater
		Chestnut-breasted Seedeater
		Chestnut Seedeater★
		Lavender-backed Finch
	collaris	Rusty-collared Seedeater
		Collared Seedeater★
		White-breasted Finch
	frontalis	Buffy-fronted Seedeater
		Cayenne Seedeater
		Euler's Seedeater
	leucoptera	White-bellied Seedeater
		Half-white Finch
	minuta	Ruddy-breasted Seedeater
		Dwarf Finch
		Lesser Seedeater
		Minute Seedeater
	nigricollis	Yellow-bellied Seedeater
		Guttural Finch
	peruviana	Parrot-billed Seedeater
		Grosbeak Seedeater
		Brown Grosbeak
	torqueola	White-collared Seedeater
		Collared Seedeater★
		Black-banded Finch
		Sharpe's Seedeater

Emberizidae: s.f. **Emberizinae** Buntings, American Sparrows (cont.)

Melopyrrha	*nigra*	Cuban Bullfinch
		Black Seed Finch
Tiaris	*bicolor*	Black-faced Grassquit
		Black-faced Cuban Finch
	canora	Melodious Grassquit
		Melodious Finch
		Cuban Finch
		Cuban Grassquit
	olivacea	Yellow-faced Grassquit
		Olive Finch
		Olive Cuban Finch
Pipilo	*erythrophthalmus*	Rufous-sided Towhee
		Red-eyed Towhee
	rutilus	Sclater's Towhee
		White-throated Towhee
Arremonops	*conirostris*	Black-striped Sparrow
		Green-backed Sparrow

(Most species of genus *Atlapetes* alternatively known as Brush Finch or Atlapetes.)

Atlapetes	*torquatus*	Stripe-headed Brush Finch
		Striped Brush Finch
Gubernatrix	*cristata*	Yellow Cardinal
		Green Cardinal
Rhodospingus	*cruentus*	Crimson Finch
		Purple-crowned Finch
		Ecuadorian Crowned Finch
		Rhodospingus Finch
Paroaria	*capitata*	Yellow-billed Cardinal
		Brazilian Cardinal
	dominicana	Red-cowled Cardinal
		Red-headed Cardinal
		Pope Cardinal
		Dominican Cardinal
	gularis	Red-capped Cardinal
		Black-throated Cardinal

Emberizidae: s.f. **Catamblyrhynchinae**   Plush-capped Finch

Catambly-	*diadema*	Plush-capped Finch
rhynchus		Plush-capped Tanager

Emberizidae: s.f. **Cardinalinae**   Cardinal-Grosbeaks

Pheucticus	*aureoventris*	Black-backed Grosbeak
		Yellow-bellied Grosbeak
		Golden-bellied Grosbeak
		Black-bellied Grosbeak
	chrysopeplus	Yellow Grosbeak
		Orange-coloured Grosbeak
Cardinalis	*cardinalis*	Cardinal
		Common Cardinal
		Virginian Cardinal
		Red Cardinal
		Scarlet Cardinal
		Crimson Cardinal
		Virginian Nightingale
	phoeniceus	Vermilion Cardinal
		Venezuelan Cardinal
		Phoenix
		Phoenix Cardinal
	sinuata	Pyrrhuloxia
		Bullfinch Cardinal
Saltator	*aurantiirostris*	Golden-billed Saltator
		Orange-billed Saltator
	maximus	Buff-throated Saltator
		Great Saltator
Passerina	*brissonii*	Ultramarine Grosbeak
		Brazilian Blue Grosbeak
	caerulea	Blue Grosbeak
		Chestnut-shouldered Blue Grosbeak
	ciris	Painted Bunting★
		Nonpareil Bunting
	leclancherii	Orange-breasted Bunting
		Rainbow Bunting
		Leclancher's Bunting
	rositae	Rose-bellied Bunting
		Rose-breasted Bunting
		Rosita Bunting
	versicolor	Varied Bunting
		Versicolour Bunting
		Painted Bunting★

FAMILY/GENUS	SPECIES/SUBSPECIES	ENGLISH NAMES

Emberizidae: s.f. **Thraupinae**   Tanagers, Honeycreepers

Nemosia	*pileata*	Hooded Tanager
		Pileated Tanager
Rhodinocicla	*rosea*	Rose-breasted Thrush Tanager
		Rosy Thrush Tanager
Creurgops	*verticalis*	Rufous-crested Tanager
		Rufous-eared Tanager
Tachyphonus	*rufus*	White-lined Tanager
		Black Tanager

(All species of genus *Habia* alternatively known as Ant Tanagers or Tanagers.)

Habia	*gutturalis*	Red-throated Ant Tanager
		Sooty Tanager
Piranga	*bidentata*	Flame-coloured Tanager
		Striped Tanager
		Swainson's Tanager
	rubra	Summer Tanager
		Cooper's Tanager
Calochaetes	*coccineus*	Vermilion Tanager
		Masked Vermilion Tanager
Ramphocelus	*bresilius*	Brazilian Tanager
		South American Scarlet Tanager
	carbo	Silver-beaked Tanager
		Maroon Tanager
	flammigerus	Flame-rumped Tanager
		Orange-rumped Tanager
	passerinii	Scarlet-rumped Tanager
		Song Tanager
		Velvet Tanager
		Passerini Tanager
Thraupis	*abbas*	Yellow-winged Tanager
		Abbot's Tanager
	bonariensis	Blue and Yellow Tanager
		Striated Tanager
	cyanoptera	Azure-shouldered Tanager
		Blue-winged Tanager
	episcopus [1]	Blue-grey Tanager
		Blue Tanager
		Silver-blue Tanager

[1] Now often shown as *virens*.

	ornata	Golden-chevroned Tanager
		Ornate Tanager
	palmarum	Palm Tanager
		Black-winged Tanager
		Olive Tanager
		Grey Tanager
Buthraupis	*rothschildi*	Golden-chested Tanager
		Rothschild's Tanager
Wetmorethraupis	*sterrhopteron*	Orange-throated Tanager
		Wetmore's Tanager
Anisognathus	*lacrymosus*	Lacrimose Mountain Tanager
		Golden Tanager
		Blue Tanager
Stephanophorus	*diadematus*	Diademed Tanager
		White-capped Tanager
Iridosornis	*jelskii*	Golden-collared Tanager
		Jelski's Tanager
	rufivertex	Golden-crowned Tanager
		Scarfed Tanager

(All species of genus *Euphonia* alternatively known as Euphonias or Tanagers.)

Euphonia	*affinis*	Scrub Euphonia
		Lesson's Euphonia
	chlorotica	Purple-throated Euphonia
		Chlorotic Euphonia
	gouldi	Olive-backed Euphonia
		Gould's Euphonia
		Gouldian Euphonia
	hirundinacea [1]	Yellow-throated Euphonia
		Bonaparte's Euphonia
		Swallow Euphonia
	imitans	Spot-crowned Euphonia
		Tawny-bellied Euphonia
	laniirostris	Thick-billed Euphonia
		Shrike-billed Euphonia
	mesochrysa	Bronze-Green Euphonia
		Bronze Euphonia
	musica	Blue-hooded Euphonia
		Blue-crowned Euphonia

---

[1] Formerly *lauta*.

Emberizidae: s.f. **Thraupinae** Tanagers, Honeycreepers (cont.)

FAMILY/GENUS	SPECIES/SUBSPECIES	ENGLISH NAMES
	violacea	Violaceous Euphonia
		Violet Euphonia
Chlorophonia	*cyanea*	Blue-naped Chlorophonia
		Blue Chlorophonia
Chlorochrysa	*phoenicotis*	Glistening Green Tanager
		Emerald Tanager
		Brown-eared Tanager
Tangara	*arthus*	Golden Tanager
		Black-eared Golden Tanager
	cabanisi	Azure-rumped Tanager
		Cabanis's Tanager
	cayana	Burnished-buff Tanager
		Rufous-crowned Tanager
		Cayenne Tanager
	cyanicollis	Blue-necked Tanager
		Blue-headed Tanager★
	cyanocephala	Red-necked Tanager
		Festive Tanager
		Blue-headed Tanager★
	cyanoptera	Black-headed Tanager
		Blue-winged Tanager
	dowii	Spangle-cheeked Tanager
		Spangled Tanager
	fastuosa	Seven-coloured Tanager
		Superb Tanager
		Green-headed Tanager
		Orange-rumped Tanager
	guttata	Speckled Tanager
		Yellow-browed Tanager
	gyrola	Bay-headed Tanager
		Chestnut-headed Tanager
		Copper-headed Tanager
		Blue-rumped Green Tanager
	inornata	Plain-coloured Tanager
		Plain Tanager
	larvata	Golden-masked Tanager
		Mrs Wilson's Tanager
		Masked Tanager★
	nigrocincta	Masked Tanager★
		Black-tinted Tanager

FAMILY/GENUS	SPECIES/SUBSPECIES	ENGLISH NAMES
	nigroviridis	Beryl-spangled Tanager
		Black and Green Tanager
		Green and Black Tanager
		Scaly Breasted Tanager
		Tiger Tanager
	parzudakii	Flame-faced Tanager
		Black-eared Tanager
	pulcherrima	Golden-collared Honeycreeper
		Golden-collared Tanager
	ruficervix	Golden-naped Tanager★
		Fawn-naped Tanager
	schrankii	Green and Gold Tanager
		Schrank's Tanager
	seledon	Green-headed Tanager
		Three-coloured Tanager
		Golden-naped Tanager★
		Celadon Tanager
	velia	Opal-rumped Tanager
		Opal Tanager

(All species of genus *Dacnis* alternatively known as Dacnis, Honeycreepers or Sugarbirds.)

FAMILY/GENUS	SPECIES/SUBSPECIES	ENGLISH NAMES
Dacnis	*berlepschi*	Scarlet-breasted Dacnis
		Berlepsch's Dacnis
	cayana	Blue Dacnis
		Turquoise Dacnis★
		Black-throated Honeycreeper
	hartlaubi	Turquoise Dacnis Tanager
		Turquoise Dacnis★
		Hartlaub's Dacnis
	lineata lineata	Black-faced Dacnis
		White-vented Dacnis
	l. egregia	Yellow-vented Dacnis
		Sulphur-bellied Honeycreeper
		Splendid Dacnis
		Egregia's Honeycreeper
Chlorophanes	*spiza*	Green Honeycreeper
		Blue Honeycreeper
		Black-headed Sugarbird

Emberizidae: s.f. **Thraupinae** Tanagers, Honeycreepers (cont.)

(All species of genus *Cyanerpes* alternatively known as Honeycreepers or Sugarbirds.)

Cyanerpes	*caeruleus*	Purple Honeycreeper
		Yellow-legged Honeycreeper
	cyaneus	Red-legged Honeycreeper
		Blue Honeycreeper
		Yellow-winged Honeycreeper

(All species of genus *Diglossa* alternatively known as Flower-Piercers or Honeycreepers.)

Diglossa	*baritula*	Slaty Flower-Piercer
		Cinnamon-bellied Flower-Piercer
		Slaty Highland Honeycreeper
	carbonaria	Carbonated Flower-Piercer
		Black Honeycreeper
	glauca	Deep-blue Flower-Piercer
		Glaucous Honeycreeper

Icteridae Blackbirds, Troupials

(Many species alternatively known as Hangnests.)

Psarocolius	*cassini*	Chestnut-mantled Oropendola
		Cassin's Oropendola
	wagleri	Chestnut-headed Oropendola
		Wagler's Oropendola
Cacicus	*holosericeus*	Yellow-billed Cacique
		Prevost's Cacique
	melanicterus	Yellow-winged Cacique
		Prevost's Mexican
	sclateri	Ecuadorean Black Cacique
		Sclater's Cacique
	solitarius	Solitary Black Cacique
		Solitary Cacique
Icterus	*chrysater*	Yellow-backed Oriole
		Lesson's Oriole
	galbula	Northern Oriole
		Baltimore Oriole [1]
		Bullock's Oriole [2]
	graduacauda	Black-headed Oriole
		Audubon's Oriole

[1] Eastern race.   [2] Western race.

FAMILY/GENUS	SPECIES/SUBSPECIES	ENGLISH NAMES
	gularis	Audubon's Black-headed Oriole
		Lichtenstein's Oriole
		Black-throated Oriole
		Altamira Oriole
	icterus	Troupial
		Common Hangnest
		Brazilian Hangnest
		Buglebird
	prosthemelas	Black-cowled Oriole
		Strickland's Oriole
	pustulatus	Scarlet-headed Oriole
		Flame-headed Oriole
		Streaked-backed Oriole
	wagleri	Black-vented Oriole
		Wagler's Oriole

(Many species of genus *Agelaius* alternatively known as Blackbirds or Marshbirds.)

FAMILY/GENUS	SPECIES/SUBSPECIES	ENGLISH NAMES
Agelaius	*icterocephalus*	Yellow-hooded Blackbird
		Yellow-headed Blackbird
	phoenicus	Red-winged Blackbird
		Redwing [1]
	tricolor	Tri-coloured Blackbird
		Tri-coloured Redwing
Leistes	*militaris*	Red-breasted Blackbird
		Red-breasted Marshbird
		Cayenne Red-breasted Marshbird
Sturnella	*defillipi*	Lesser Red-breasted Meadowlark
		Filippi's Red-breasted Meadowlark
	loyca	Long-tailed Meadowlark
		Military Starling [2]
		Red-breasted Starling
		Patagonian Marsh Starling
	magna	Eastern Meadowlark
		Western Meadowlark
Pseudoleistes	*virescens*	Brown and Yellow Marshbird
		Brown-rumped Marshbird
Dives	*dives*	Melodious Blackbird
		Singing Blackbird
		Sumichrast Blackbird

[1] Not synonymous with *Turdus iliacus* – Eurasian Redwing.　　[2] Formerly *Pezites militaris*.

Icteridae Blackbirds, Troupials (cont.)

Quiscalus	*quiscula*	Common Grackle
		Purple Grackle
Molothrus	*aeneus*	Bronzed Cowbird
		Red-eyed Cowbird
		Brown Cowbird
	ater	Brown-headed Cowbird
		Common Cowbird★
	badius	Bay-winged Cowbird
		Bay-headed Cowbird
	bonariensis	Shiny Cowbird
		Silky Cowbird
		Glossy Cowbird
		Common Cowbird★
Scaphidura	*oryzivora*	Giant Cowbird
		Rice Cowbird

Fringillidae: s.f. **Fringillinae**   Chaffinches, Brambling

Fringilla	*montifringilla*	Brambling
		Bramble Finch
		Mountain Finch
		Royal Chaffinch
	teydea	Canary Islands Chaffinch
		Blue Chaffinch

Fringillidae: s.f. **Carduelinae**   Goldfinches and Allied Finches
(Many species of genus *Serinus* alternatively known as Serins, Canaries, Seedeaters or Singing Finches.)

Serinus	*alario*	Black-head Canary
		Black-headed Canary
		Mountain Canary★
		Alario Finch
	albogularis	White-throated Seedeater
		White-headed Seedeater
	atrogularis	Black-throated Canary
		Angolan Singing Finch
		Yellow-rumped Seedeater
		Peach Canary
	burtoni	Grosbeak Seedeater
		Thick-billed Seedeater
	canicollis	Yellow-crowned Canary

		Cape Canary*
		Grey-necked Serin
	citrinella	Citril Finch
		Mountain Finch*
	flaviventris	Yellow Canary
		St Helena Seedeater
		Yellow-bellied Seedeater
	leucopterus	White-winged Seedeater
		Dusky-faced Seedeater
		Layard's Seedeater
		Protea Canary
	leucopygius	White-rumped Seedeater
		Grey Singing Finch
		Grey Canary
	mennelli	Black-eared Seedeater
		Mennell's Canary
	mozambicus	Yellow-fronted Canary
		Green Singing Finch
		Yellow-eyed Canary
		Icterine Canary
		Mozambique Serin
		Shelley
	nigriceps	Black-headed Serin
		Rüppell's Siskin
	pusillus	Gold-fronted Serin
		Orange-fronted Serin
		Red-fronted Serin
		Red-capped Serin
		Gold-fronted Finch
	reichardi	Reichard's Seedeater
		Stripe-breasted Seedeater
	scotops	Forest Canary
		Striped Canary
		Sundevall's Canary
		Natal Linnet
		Grass Shelley
	sulphuratus	Brimstone Canary
		Bully Canary
		Sulphury Seedeater
		Sulphur-coloured Seedeater
	symondsi	Symond's Cape Siskin

Fringillidae: s.f. **Carduelinae** Goldfinches and Allied Finches (cont.)

		Drakensberg Siskin
	totta totta	Cape Siskin
		Cape Canary★
		Totta Siskin
		Rock Canary
		South African Siskin
		Siskin Canary
	t. symonsi	Mountain Siskin
		Brown Canary
		Drakenberg Siskin
Neospiza	*concolor*	Sao Thomé Grosbeak
		Grosbeak Weaver★
Carduelis	*ambigua*	Oustalet's Black-headed Greenfinch
		Black-headed Greenfinch★
	cucullatus	Red Siskin
		Red Hooded Siskin
		Black-hooded Red Siskin
		Hooded Siskin★
	magellanicus	Hooded Siskin★
		Southern Siskin
		Magellan Siskin
		Black-headed Siskin★
	psaltria	Lesser Goldfinch
		Dark-backed Siskin
		Green-backed Siskin
		Arkansas Siskin
	sinica	Oriental Greenfinch
		Chinese Greenfinch
		Grey-capped Greenfinch
	spinoides	Black-headed Greenfinch★
		Himalayan Greenfinch
		Himalayan Siskin
		Yellow-breasted Greenfinch
	uropygialis	Yellow-rumped Siskin
		Mountain Canary★
	yarrellii	Yellow-faced Siskin
		Yarrell's Siskin
		Yarrell's Goldfinch
Acanthis	*hornemanni*	Hoary Redpoll
		Arctic Redpoll

FAMILY/GENUS	SPECIES/SUBSPECIES	ENGLISH NAMES
Leucosticte	*arctoa*	Rosy Finch
		Grey-crowned Rosy Finch
	nemoricola	Hodgson's Rosy Finch
		Plain Mountain Finch
Rhodopechys	*githaginea*	Trumpeter Finch
		Trumpeter Bullfinch
Carpodacus	*edwardsii*	Large Rosefinch
		Dark-rumped Rosefinch
		Edward's Rosefinch
	eos	Stresemann's Rosefinch
		Pink-rumped Rosefinch
		Dawn Rosefinch
	erythrinus	Scarlet Grosbeak
		Rosefinch
		Common Rosefinch
Carpodacus	*mexicanus*	House Finch
		Mexican Rosefinch
	nipalensis	Dark Rosefinch
		Dark-breasted Rosefinch
	puniceus	Red-breasted Rosefinch
		Red-fronted Rosefinch
	purpureus	Purple Finch
		Purple Rosefinch
	rhodopeplus	Spotted Rosefinch
		Spot-winged Rosefinch
		Pink-browed Rosefinch
	rubicilloides	Streaked Great Rosefinch
		Crimson-eared Rosefinch
	thura	Mlle Thura's Rosefinch
		White-browed Rosefinch
Pinicola	*subhimachala*	Red-headed Finch
		Crimson-browed Finch
Loxia	*curvirostra*	Red Crossbill
		Crossbill
		Common Crossbill
		Scarlet Crossbill
		Spruce Crossbill
	leucoptera	White-winged Crossbill
		Two-barred Crossbill
Pyrrhula	*erythaca*	Beavan's Bullfinch
		Grey-headed Bullfinch

Fringillidae: s.f. **Carduelinae** Goldfinches and Allied Finches (cont.)

		Red-breasted Bullfinch
Coccothraustes	*affinis*	Allied Grosbeak
		Collared Grosbeak
	migratorius	Black-tailed Hawfinch
		Black-headed Hawfinch★
		Lesser Black-headed Hawfinch
		Chinese Hawfinch
		Asiatic Hawfinch
		Japanese Hawfinch [1]
		Yellow-billed Hawfinch
		Yellow-billed Grosbeak★
	personatus	Masked Hawfinch
		Japanese Masked Hawfinch
		Japanese Hawfinch
		Japanese Grosbeak
		Masked Grosbeak
		Black-headed Hawfinch★
		Greater Black-headed Hawfinch
		Yellow-billed Grosbeak★

Estrildidae   Waxbills

Parmoptila	*woodhousei*	Flower-pecker Weaver Finch
		Woodhouse's Antpecker
Nigrita	*canicapilla*	Grey-headed Negro Finch
		Grey-breasted Negro Finch
Nesocharis	*capistrata*	White-cheeked Olive Weaver
		Grey-crowned Oliveback
		Grey-headed Oliveback
	shelleyi	Little Olive Weaver
		Little Olive Waxbill
Pytilia	*afra*	Orange-winged Pytilia
		Red-faced Finch
		Red-faced Waxbill
		Golden-backed Pytilia
	hypogrammica	Yellow-winged Pytilia
		Red-faced Aurora Waxbill
	melba	Green-winged Pytilia
		Melba Finch

---

[1] Wrongly named as this species is confined to a limited area of China.

FAMILY/GENUS	SPECIES/SUBSPECIES	ENGLISH NAMES
		Crimson-faced Waxbill
	phoenicoptera	Red-winged Pytilia
		Red-winged Waxbill
		Crimson-winged Waxbill
		Crimson-winged Pytilia
		Aurora Finch
Mandingoa	*nitidulus*	Green-backed Twin-spot
		Green Twin-spot
Cryptospiza	*jacksoni*	Dusky Crimson-wing
		Jackson's Crimson-wing
		Jackson's Forest Finch
	reichenovii	Red-faced Crimson-wing
		Red-eyed Crimson-wing
		Forest Finch
		Reichenow's Crimson-wing
	salvadorii	Abyssinian Crimson-wing
		Salvadori's Crimson-wing
Pirenestes	*minor*	Nyasa Seed-cracker
		Lesser Seed-cracker
	ostrinus	Black-bellied Seed-cracker
		Seed-cracker
		Thick-billed Forest Weaver
Spermophaga	*haematina*	Blue-billed Weaver
		Western Blue-bill
		Red-breasted Blue-bill
		Crimson-breasted Weaver
Hypargos	*margaritatus*	Rosy Twin-spot
		Verreaux's Twin-spot
		Pink-throated Twin-spot
	niveoguttatus	Peter's Twin-spot
		Red-throated Twin-spot
		Peter's Spotted Firefinch
Lagonosticta	*lavarta*	Black-faced Firefinch
		Black-throated Firefinch
		Masked Firefinch
	rara	Black-bellied Firefinch
		Black-bellied Waxbill
	rhodopareia	Jameson's Firefinch
		Abyssinian Firefinch

Estrildidae Waxbills (cont.)

		Pink-backed Firefinch
	rubricata	African Firefinch
		Dark Firefinch
		Brown-backed Firefinch
		Black-vented Crimson Firefinch
		Blue-billed Firefinch
		Ruddy Waxbill
	senegala	Red-billed Firefinch
		Firefinch
		Common Firefinch
		Senegal Firefinch
Uraeginthus	*angolensis*	Angolan Cordon-Bleu
		Blue-breasted Cordon-Bleu
		Blue-breasted Waxbill
		Southern Blue Waxbill
		Blue Waxbill
	bengalus	Red-cheeked Cordon-Bleu
		Cordon-Bleu
		Red-cheeked Blue Waxbill
	cyanocephala	Blue-capped Cordon-Bleu
		Blue-headed Cordon-Bleu
		Blue-capped Waxbill
		Blue-headed Waxbill
	granatina	Violet-eared Cordon-Bleu
		Violet-eared Waxbill
		Grenadier Waxbill★
		Grenadier
		Common Grenadier
	ianthinogaster	Purple Grenadier
		Grenadier Waxbill★
		Purple-bellied Waxbill
Estrilda	*astrild*	Waxbill
		Common Waxbill★
		St Helena Waxbill
		Barred Waxbill
		Brown Waxbill
		Pheasant Finch
		Red-bellied Waxbill
	atricapilla	Black-headed Waxbill
		Black-capped Waxbill

	caerulescens	Bluish Waxbill
		Lavender Waxbill★
		Grey Waxbill★
		Lavender Finch
		Red-tailed Lavender Finch
	erythronotos	Black-cheeked Waxbill
		Black-faced Waxbill
	melanotis melanotis	Yellow-bellied Waxbill
		Dufresne's Waxbill
		Swee Waxbill
	nigriloris	Black-lored Waxbill
		Black-faced Waxbill
		Kiabo Waxbill
	perreini	Lavender Waxbill★
		Black-tailed Lavender Waxbill
		Black-tailed Lavender Finch
		Black-tailed Grey Waxbill
		Grey Waxbill
	rhodopyga	Crimson-rumped Waxbill
		Rosy-rumped Waxbill
		Rosy-winged Waxbill
		Crimson-winged Waxbill
		Sundevall's Waxbill
		Ruddy Waxbill
	thomensis	Neumann's Waxbill
		Angola Waxbill
		Cinderella Waxbill
	troglodytes	Black-rumped Waxbill
		Red-eared Waxbill
		Common Waxbill★
		Pink-cheeked Waxbill
		Grey Waxbill★
		Grey-rumped Waxbill
Aegintha	*temporalis*	Red-browed Finch
		Red-browed Waxbill
		Sydney Waxbill
		Temporal Finch
		Red-head
Amandava	*amandava*	Red Avadavat
		Strawberry Finch
		Tiger Finch

Estrildidae Waxbills (cont.)

		Red Waxbill
		Red Munia
		Bombay Avadavat
	formosa	Green Avadavat
		Green Munia
	subflava	Zebra Waxbill
		Golden-breasted Waxbill
		Gold-breast Waxbill
		Orange-breasted Waxbill
		Orange Waxbill
Ortygospiza	*atricollis*	Black-chinned Quail Finch
		Quail Finch
		Common Quail Finch
		African Quail Finch
	gabonensis	Gabon Quail Finch
		Red-billed Quail Finch
		Black-chinned Quail Finch
Emblema	*bella*	Beautiful Firetail
		Firetail Finch
	guttata	Diamond Firetail
		Diamond Fire-tailed Finch
		Diamond Sparrow
		Diamond Finch
		Spot-sided Finch
	oculata	Red-eared Firetail
		Red-eared Finch
	picta	Painted Finch★
		Painted Firetail
		Mountain Finch★
Neochmia	*phaeton phaeton*	Crimson Finch
		Blood Finch
		Australian Firefinch
	p. albiventer	White-bellied Crimson Finch
		Pale Crimson Finch
	ruficauda	Star Finch
		Ruficauda Finch
		Red-faced Finch
		Red-tailed Finch
		Rufous-tailed Finch
		Weaver Finch

FAMILY/GENUS	SPECIES/SUBSPECIES	ENGLISH NAMES
		Red-tailed Grass Finch
Poephila	*acuticauda*	Long-tailed Finch
		Long-tailed Grass Finch
	bichenovii bichenovii	Banded Finch
		Bicheno Finch
		Bicheno
		White-rumped Bicheno
		Owl Finch
		Double-barred Finch
		Double-bar Finch
	b. annulosa	Double-barred Finch
		Black-ringed Finch
		Black-rumped Bicheno
		Black-rumped Finch
		Black-winged Finch
	cincta cincta	Black-throated Finch
		Parson Finch
	c. atropygialis	Black-rumped Parson Finch
		Black-tailed Finch
		Diggle's Finch
	personata	Masked Finch
		Masked Grass Finch
Erythrura	*coloria*	Mindanao Parrot Finch
		Red-eared Parrot Finch
		Red-collared Parrot Finch
		Many-coloured Parrot Finch
		Mount Katanglad Parrot Finch
	cyanovirens	
	cyanovirens	Red-headed Parrot Finch★
		Blue-bellied Parrot Finch
		Blue and Green Parrot Finch
		Parrot Finch
	c. pealei	Peale's Parrot Finch
		Fijian Parrot Finch
	hyperythra	Green-tailed Parrot Finch
		Tawny-breasted Parrot Finch
		Bamboo Parrot Finch
		Mountain Parrot Finch
		Green-rumped Parrot Finch
		Bamboo Munia
	kleinschmidti	Kleinschmidt's Parrot Finch

Estrildidae Waxbills (cont.)

		Pink-billed Parrot Finch
		Black-faced Parrot Finch
	prasina	Long-tailed Munia
		Pin-tailed Nonpareil
		Pin-tailed Parrot Finch
		Nonpareil Parrot Finch
		Red-bellied Munia
	psittacea	Red-throated Parrot Finch
		Red-headed Parrot Finch★
		Parrot Finch
		Red-faced Parrot Finch
	trichroa	Blue-faced Parrot Finch
		Blue-faced Finch
		Green-backed Finch
		Tri-coloured Parrot Finch★
		Three-coloured Parrot Finch★
	tricolor	Timor Parrot Finch
		Three-coloured Parrot Finch★
		Tri-coloured Parrot Finch★
		Blue-breasted Parrot Finch
		Blue-fronted Parrot Finch
	viridifacies	Green-faced Parrot Finch
		Green-headed Parrot Finch
		Manila Parrot Finch
Chloebia	*gouldiae*	Gouldian Finch
		Lady Gould's Finch
		Purple-breasted Finch
		Rainbow Finch
		Painted Finch★
Aidemosyne	*modesta*	Plum-headed Finch
		Plum-capped Finch
		Cherry Finch
		Modest Finch
		Plain-coloured Finch
		Diadem Finch

(Asian species of genus *Lonchura* alternatively known as Mannikins, Munias
or Nuns.)

Lonchura	*bicolor*	Black-and-White Mannikin
		Fernando Po Mannikin [1]

---

[1] Name should be reserved for subspecies.

	Black-breasted Mannikin
	Red-backed Mannikin
	Blue-billed Mannikin
caniceps	Pearl-headed Silverbill★
	Grey-headed Silverbill★
	Grey-headed Mannikin [1]
castaneothorax	Chestnut-breasted Mannikin
	Chestnut-breasted Finch
	Chestnut Finch
cucullata	Bronze Mannikin
	Bronze-winged Mannikin
	Bronzewing
	Hooded Finch
flaviprymna	Yellow-tailed Finch
	Yellow-rumped Finch
	Yellow-rumped Mannikin
fringilloides	Magpie Mannikin
	Pied Mannikin
fuscans	Dusky Mannikin
	Brown Mannikin
grandis	Great-billed Mannikin
	Great Munia
	Grand-billed Munia
	Grand Munia
griseicapilla	Pearl-headed Silverbill★
	Grey-headed Silverbill★
kelaarti	Jerdon's Mannikin
	Rufous-bellied Munia
	Ceylon Hill Munia
leucogastra	White-breasted Mannikin
	White-bellied Munia
leucogastroides	Javanese Mannikin
	Black-rumped Munia
	Black-beaked Bronze Mannikin
maja maja	White-headed Mannikin
	Pale-headed Mannikin★
	Maja Finch
	Maja Munia

---

[1] *L. caniceps* usually known as Silverbill, Grey-headed Mannikin being more appropriate to subspecies of *L. maja*.

Estrildidae Waxbills (cont.)

m. ferruginosa	Javan White-headed Munia
	Black-throated Munia
	Javan Maja Munia
	Javan Munia
malabarica	
malabarica	Silverbill
	Indian Silverbill
	Common Silverbill
	White-rumped Munia
	White-throated Munia
	Plain Brown Munia
m. cantans	Silverbill
	African Silverbill
	Common Silverbill
	Warbling Silverbill
malacca malacca	Tri-coloured Nun
	Three-coloured Mannikin
m. atricapilla	Black-headed Nun
	Chestnut-bellied Nun
	Chestnut Mannikin
melaena	New Britain Mannikin
	Brown's Mannikin
nana	Madagascar Mannikin
	Dwarf Mannikin
	Bib Finch
	Nana
nevermanni	White-crowned Mannikin
	Grey-crowned Mannikin
pallida	Pale-headed Mannikin*
	Grey-headed Mannikin
	Pallid Munia
	Pale Sunda Munia
pectoralis	Pectoralis Finch
	Pectoral Finch
	Pictorella Finch
	Pectoralis Mannikin
	White-breasted Finch
	White-breasted Munia
punctulata	Spotted Munia
	Spice Mannikin

		Spice Finch
		Spicebird
		Nutmeg Finch
		Nutmeg Mannikin
		Mascot Finch
		Scaly-breasted Munia
		Common Munia
	quinticolor	Sunda Munia
		Chestnut and White Munia
		Lesser Sunda Munia
		Five-coloured Mannikin
	spectabilis	New Britain Mannikin
		Sclater's Mannikin
		Hooded Mannikin
	striata striata	White-rumped Munia
		White-backed Munia
		Striated Munia
	s. acuticauda	Sharp-tailed Munia
		Sharp-tailed Finch
		Hodgson's Munia
Padda	*fuscata*	Timor Sparrow
		Timor Ricebird
		Timor Dusky Sparrow
	oryzivora	Java Sparrow
		Rice Bird
		Rice Munia
		Paddy Bird
		Temple Bird
Amadina	*erythrocephala*	Red-headed Finch
		Red-headed Amadina
		Red-headed Weaver Finch
		Paradise Sparrow
	fasciata	Cut-Throat
		Cut-throat Finch
		Cut-throat Weaver
		Ribbon Finch
		Ribbon Weaver Finch
		Cut-throat Amadina

Ploceidae: s.f. Viduinae   Parasitic Whydahs
(Many species alternatively known as Whydahs, Widowbirds or Widow Finches.)

Vidua	*chalybeata*	Indigo Bird
		Green Indigo Bird
		Purple Indigo Bird
		Senegal Indigo Bird
		Steel Finch*
		Steel-blue Widow Finch
		Combassou
		Senegal Combassou
	fischeri	Fischer's Whydah
		Straw-tailed Whydah
	funerea	Dusky Indigo Bird
		Steel Finch*
		Black Indigo Bird
	hypocherina	Steel-blue Whydah
		Long-tailed Combassou
		Resplendent Combassou
	orientalis	Broad-tailed Paradise Whydah
		Broad-tailed Whydah
	regia	Shaft-tailed Whydah
		Queen Whydah

Ploceidae: s.f. Ploceinae   Weavers, Sparrows

Bubalornis	*albirostris*	Buffalo Weaver
		Black Buffalo Weaver
		White-billed Buffalo Weaver
Dinemellia	*dinemelli*	White-headed Buffalo Weaver
		Dinemelli's Buffalo Weaver
		Dinemelli's Weaver
Plocepasser	*mahali*	Stripe-breasted Sparrow Weaver
		White-browed Sparrow Weaver
		Mahali Weaver
	rufoscapularis	Rufous-backed Sparrow Weaver
		Chestnut-backed Sparrow Weaver
		Chestnut-mantled Sparrow Weaver
Philetairus	*socius*	Social Weaver
		Sociable Weaver
Passer	*flaveolus*	Pegu House Sparrow
		Plain-backed Sparrow

FAMILY/GENUS	SPECIES/SUBSPECIES	ENGLISH NAMES
	iagoensis	Rufous-backed Sparrow
		Great Sparrow
	luteus	Golden Sparrow
		Golden Song Sparrow
		Sudan Golden Song Sparrow
		Yellow Sparrow
	moabiticus	Dead Sea Sparrow
		Scrub Sparrow
	rutilans	Cinnamon Sparrow
		Russet Sparrow
Petronia	*dentata*	Bush Petronia
		Bush Sparrow
		Lesser Rock Sparrow
		South African Rock Sparrow
	petronia	Rock Sparrow
		Petronia
	xanthocollis	Yellow-throated Sparrow
		Yellow-throated Rock Sparrow
		Yellow-throated Petronia

(Many species of genus *Montifringilla* alternatively known as Snow Finches or Finches.)

Montifringilla	*ruficollis*	Red-necked Snow Finch
		Rufous-necked Snow Finch
	taczanowskii	White-rumped Snow Finch
		Taczanowski's Snow Finch
	theresae	Theresa's Snow Finch
		Meinerthagen's Snow Finch
Sporopipes	*frontalis*	Speckle-fronted Weaver
		Scaly-fronted Weaver★
		Speckled Weaver
		Red-fronted Finch
	squamifrons	Scaly-fronted Weaver★
		Scaly-crowned Weaver
		Scaly Weaver
Amblyospiza	*albifrons*	Grosbeak Weaver
		White-fronted Grosbeak
		Thick-billed Weaver
		Hawfinch Weaver
		White-fronted Weaver

Ploceidae: s.f. **Ploceinae** Weavers, Sparrows (cont.)

(Some species of genus *Ploceus* alternatively known as Golden Weavers or Weavers.)

Ploceus	*albinucha*	White-naped Black Weaver
		Black Weaver
	benghalensis	Black-throated Weaver Bird
		Black-breasted Weaver
		Bengal Weaver
	bicolor	Dark-backed Weaver
		Forest Weaver
	bojeri	Golden Palm Weaver
		Mombasa Golden Weaver
		Bojer's Weaver
	cucullatus cucullatus	Black-headed Weaver*
		Village Weaver
		Spotted-backed Weaver
		Rufous-necked Weaver
		Golden Oriole Weaver
		V-marked Weaver
	c. abyssinicus	Abyssinian Black-headed Weaver
		Great Masked Weaver
	dichrocephalus	Jubaland Weaver
		Yellow-backed Weaver*
	flavipes	Yellow-footed Weaver
		Yellow-legged Weaver
	intermedius	Masked Weaver
		Lesser Masked Weaver
	jacksoni	Golden-backed Weaver
		Jackson's Weaver
	luteolus	Little Weaver*
		Slender-billed Weaver*
		Little Masked Weaver
		Atlas Weaver
	manyar	Streaked Weaver
		Striated Weaver
		Manyar Weaver
		Javan Weaver
	megarhynchus	Finn's Baya
		Yellow Weaver
	melanocephalus	Yellow-backed Weaver*
		Black-headed Weaver*

FAMILY/GENUS	SPECIES/SUBSPECIES	ENGLISH NAMES
	melanogaster	Black Mountain Weaver
		Black-billed Weaver
	nigricollis	Black-necked Weaver
		Spectacled Weaver★
	nigrimentum	Angola Weaver
		Black-chinned Weaver
	pelzelni	Slender-billed Weaver★
		Little Weaver★
		Pelzeln's Weaver
	rubiginosus	Chestnut Weaver
		Chocolate Weaver
	subaureus	Olive-headed Golden Weaver
		Golden Weaver
		Smith's Golden Weaver
	subpersonatus	Western Golden Weaver
		Loango Weaver
	velatus	Vitelline Masked Weaver
		Southern Masked Weaver
		Greater Masked Weaver
		African Masked Weaver
		Namaqua Masked Weaver
		Half-masked Weaver
		Black-fronted Weaver
		Ruppell's Weaver★
	xanthops	Holub's Golden Weaver
		Large Golden Weaver
	xanthopterus	Southern Brown-throated Weaver
		Brown-throated Golden Weaver
Quelea	*erythrops*	Red-headed Quelea
		Red-headed Dioch
		Red-headed Weaver★
	quelea	Red-billed Quelea
		Red-billed Weaver
		Black-faced Dioch
		Sudan Dioch
		Common Dioch
		Common Quelea
		Weaver Finch
Foudia	*eminentissimo*	Red Forest Fody
		Red-headed Forest Fody
	madagascariensis	Madagascar Fody
		Madagascar Weaver

FAMILY/GENUS   SPECIES/SUBSPECIES   ENGLISH NAMES

Ploceidae: s.f. **Ploceinae** Weavers, Sparrows (cont.)
(Long-tailed species of genus *Euplectes* alternatively known as Whydahs or
Widowbirds. The short-tailed species generally alternatively known as
Weavers or Bishops, but there are exceptions.)

Euplectes	*afer*	Yellow-crowned Bishop
		Golden Bishop
		Napolean Weaver
	anomalus	Anomalus Bishop
		Bob-tailed Weaver
	ardens	Red-collared Widowbird
		Cut-throat Whydah
		Black Whydah
		Long-tailed Black Whydah
	axillaris	Fan-tailed Widowbird
		Red-shouldered Whydah
	capensis	Yellow Bishop
		Black and Yellow Bishop
		Yellow-rumped Bishop
		Yellow-rumped Whydah
		Yellow-backed Weaver
		Yellow-shouldered Weaver
		Cape Weaver
	franciscanus [1]	West African Red Bishop
		Orange Weaver
		Fire-crowned Weaver
	gierowii	Black Bishop
		Gierow's Bishop
	hordeaceus	Black-winged Red Bishop
		Black-winged Bishop
		Fire-crowned Bishop
		Crimson-crowned Bishop
		Red-crowned Bishop
	macrourus	Yellow-mantled Whydah
		Yellow-backed Whydah
		Gold-backed Whydah
		Gold-mantled Whydah
	nigroventris	Black-vented Widowbird
		Black-bellied Weaver
		Black-bellied Grenadier

[1] Now usually regarded as subspecies of *E. orix*.

FAMILY/GENUS	SPECIES/SUBSPECIES	ENGLISH NAMES

		Zanzibar Bishop
		Zanzibar Red Bishop
	orix	Red Bishop
		Crimson Weaver
		Red Kaffir Finch
		Orix Bishop
		Grenadier Weaver
		Red Grenadier
		Crimson Grenadier
		Scarlet Grenadier
	progne	Long-tailed Widowbird
		Giant Whydah
Anomalospiza	imberbis	Parasitic Weaver
		Cuckoo Weaver

Sturnidae Starlings

Aplonis	cantoroides	Little Starling
		Singing Glossy Starling
	metallicus	Colonial Starling
		Shining Starling
		Metallic Starling
		Shining Calornis
	panayensis	Glossy Starling
		Philippine Glossy Starling
		Greater Glossy Starling
		Asia Green Starling
		Asiatic Glossy Starling
		Glossy Calornis
	striatus	Striped Glossy Starling
		Striated Starling

(Most species of genus *Onycognathus* alternatively known as Red-winged Starling or Chestnut-winged Starling.)

Onycognathus	morio	Red-winged Starling
		Crag Chestnut-winged Starling
	salvadorii	Bristle-crowned Starling
		Crowned Starling
	tristramii	Tristram's Starling
		Tristram's Grackle

177

Sturnidae Starlings (cont.)
(All species of genus *Lamprotornis* are generally known as Glossy Starlings or Long-tailed Glossy Starlings, but are sometimes shown as just Starlings.)

Lamprotornis	*acuticaudus*	Wedge-tailed Glossy Starling
		Sharp-tailed Glossy Starling
	australis	Burchell's Glossy Starling
		Greater Glossy Starling
	chalcurus	Short-tailed Glossy Starling
		Bronze-tailed Glossy Starling
	chalybaeus	Blue-eared Glossy Starling
		Green Glossy Starling
		Green-winged Glossy Starling
		Greater Blue-eared Glossy Starling
	chloropterus	Swainson's Glossy Starling
		Lesser Blue-eared Glossy Starling
	corruscus	Black-breasted Glossy Starling
		Black-bellied Glossy Starling
	iris	Emerald Starling
		Iris Glossy Starling
	mevesii	Meves's Long-tailed Glossy Starling
		Long-tailed Purple Starling
		Meves's Starling
	ornatus	Principe Glossy Starling
		Choucador Starling
		Ornate Starling
	purpureiceps	Purple-headed Glossy Starling★
		Velvet-headed Glossy Starling
	purpureus	Purple Glossy Starling
		Purple-headed Glossy Starling★
Cinnyricinclus	*leucogaster*	Violet-backed Starling
		Violet Starling
		Amethyst Starling
		White-bellied Amethyst Starling
		White-bellied Starling
		Plum-coloured Starling
Neocichla	*gutturalis*	White-winged Babbling Starling
		White-winged Starling
		Babbling Starling
Spreo	*hildebrandti*	Hildebrandt's Starling
		Chestnut-bellied Starling
	regius	Golden-breasted Starling

		Regal Starling
		Royal Starling
	superbus	Superb Starling
		Superb Spreo Starling
		Superb Spreo
		Superb Glossy Starling
		Spreo Glossy Starling
Creatophora	*cinerea*	Wattled Starling
		Locustbird

(Many species of genus *Sturnus*, particularly those of Indian subcontinent, alternatively known as Starlings or Mynahs.)

Sturnus	*burmannicus*	Jerdon's Starling
		Vineous-breasted Starling
	cineraceus	Grey Starling
		Ashy Starling
		White-cheeked Starling
	contra	Pied Starling
		Asian Pied Starling
		Bare-eyed Starling
		Pied Mynah
	erythropygius	White-headed Starling
		Andaman Starling
	malabaricus	Grey-headed Starling
		Ashy-headed Starling
		Chestnut-faced Starling
		Chestnut-tailed Starling
		Malabar Mynah
	nigricollis	Black-collared Starling
		Black-necked Starling
	pagodarum	Brahminy Starling
		Pagoda Starling
	philippensis	Red-cheeked Starling
		Violet-backed Starling
	roseus	Rose-coloured Starling
		Rosy Starling
		Rosy Pastor
	senex	Ceylon White-headed Starling
		White-faced Starling
	sericeus	Silky Starling
		Red-billed Starling
	sinensis	Grey-backed Starling

Sturnidae Starlings (cont.)

FAMILY/GENUS	SPECIES/SUBSPECIES	ENGLISH NAMES
		White-shouldered Starling
		Chinese Mynah
		Mandarin Mynah
	sturninus	Daurian Starling
		Purple-backed Starling
Leucopsar	*rothschildi*	Rothschild's Mynah
		Rothschild's Starling
		Rothschild's Grackle
		Bali Mynah
		Bali Starling
		White Starling
Acridotheres	*cristatellus*	Crested Mynah
		Tufted Mynah
		Chinese Crested Mynah
		Chinese Jungle Mynah
	fuscus	Jungle Mynah
		Brown Mynah
	ginginianus	Bank Mynah
		Indian Mynah★
		Maldive Mynah
	grandis	Great Mynah
		Orange-billed Mynah
	tristis	Common Mynah
		Indian Mynah★

(All species of genera *Mino* and *Basilornis* alternatively known as Mynahs, Grackles or Starlings.)

FAMILY/GENUS	SPECIES/SUBSPECIES	ENGLISH NAMES
Mino	*dumonti*	Yellow-faced Mynah
		Papuan Mynah
		Dumonti's Mynah
Basilornis	*celebensis*	Celebes Starling
		King Starling
	corythaix	Moluccan Starling
		Ceram Starling
	galeatus	Sula Starling★
		Crested Starling
Streptocitta	*albertinae*	Albertina's Starling
		Sula Starling★
	albicollis	New Caledonian Starling
		Buton Starling
		Celebes Magpie

FAMILY/GENUS	SPECIES/SUBSPECIES	ENGLISH NAMES
Sarcops	*calvus*	Bald Starling
		Bald-headed Starling
		Coleto Starling
		Coleto Mynah
		Coleto
Gracula	*religiosa religiosa*	Hill Mynah
		Greater Hill Mynah
		Javan Hill Mynah
	r. indica	Southern Hill Mynah
		Lesser Hill Mynah
	r. intermedia	Assam Hill Mynah
		Nepal Hill Mynah

Oriolidae Old World Orioles

Oriolus	*crassirostris*	Sao Thomé Oriole
		Great-billed Oriole
	cruentus	Crimson-breasted Oriole
		Black and Crimson Oriole
	flavocinctus	Green Oriole
		Yellow Oriole
	forsteni	Forsten's Oriole
		Ceram Oriole
	mellianus	Mell's Maroon Oriole
		Silver Oriole
	monacha	Black-headed Forest Oriole
		Dark-head Oriole
		Forest Oriole
	phaeochromus	Ruddy Oriole
		Moluccan Oriole
		Halmahera Oriole
	sagittatus	White-bellied Oriole
		Olive-backed Oriole
	viridifuscus	Dark Oriole
		Timor Oriole

Dicruridae Drongos

Dicrurus	*adsimilis*	Fork-tailed Drongo
		Drongo
		Black Drongo
		Glossy-backed Drongo
	hottentottus	Hair-crested Drongo

Dicruridae Drongos (cont.)

	Spangled Drongo
paradiseus	Greater Racket-tailed Drongo
	Racket-tailed Drongo
	Large Racket-tailed Drongo

Cracticidae Butcherbirds

Cracticus   *mentalis*   White-throated Butcherbird
                              Black-backed Butcherbird

Ptilonorhynchidae Bowerbirds

Ailuroedus   *melanotis*   Green Catbird
                              Black-eared Catbird
                              Spotted Catbird

Scenopoeetes *dentirostris*   Tooth-billed Bowerbird
                              Stage-maker

(All species of genus *Amblyornis* alternatively known as Gardener Bowerbirds or Gardeners.)

Amblyornis   *inornatus*   Gardener Bowerbird
                              Crestless Gardener
             macgregoriae   MacGregor's Bowerbird
                              MacGregor's Gardener Bowerbird
             subalaris   Striped Bowerbird
                              Orange-crested Gardener

Prionodura   *newtoniana*   Golden Bowerbird
                              Newton's Bowerbird

Sericulus   *aureus*   New Guinea Golden Bowerbird
                              Black-faced Golden Bowerbird
                              Golden Regent Bowerbird
             bakeri   Beck's Bowerbird
                              Adelbert Regent Bowerbird
                              Adelbert Bowerbird

Chlamydera   *lauterbachi*   Yellow-breasted Bowerbird
                              Lauterbach's Bowerbird
             nuchalis   Great Bowerbird
                              Great Grey Bowerbird

Paradisaeidae Birds of Paradise

Loboparadisea *sericea*   Yellow-breasted Bird of Paradise
                              Wattle-billed Bird of Paradise

Cnemophilus *macgregorii*   Multi-crested Bird of Paradise

FAMILY/GENUS	SPECIES/SUBSPECIES	ENGLISH NAMES
		Sickle-crested Bird of Paradise
Macgregoria	*pulchra*	MacGregor's Bird of Paradise
		Moluccan Bird of Paradise
Lycocorax	*pyrrhopterus*	Brown-winged Bird of Paradise
		Paradise Crow
		Silky Crow

(All species of genus *Manucodia* alternatively known as Birds of Paradise or Manucodes.)

FAMILY/GENUS	SPECIES/SUBSPECIES	ENGLISH NAMES
Manucodia	*chalybatus*	Green-breasted Manucode
		Crinkle-collared Manucode
	comrii	Curl-breasted Manucode
		Curl-crested Manucode
Ptiloris	*victoriae*	Victoria Riflebird
		Queen Victoria Riflebird
Semioptera	*wallacei*	Standard-winged Bird of Paradise
		Wallace's Standard-winged Bird of Paradise
		Wallace's Standard-wing
Drepanornis	*albertisii*	Black-billed Sicklebill Bird of Paradise
		D'Albertis's Bird of Paradise
	bruijnii	White-billed Sicklebill Bird of Paradise
		Bruijn's Bird of Paradise
Epimachus	*fastuosus*	Black Sickle-billed Bird of Paradise
		Black Sicklebill
	meyeri	Brown Sickle-billed Bird of Paradise
		Meyer's Sickle-billed Bird of Paradise
		Long-tailed Sicklebill
		Brown Sicklebill

(All species of genus *Astrapia* alternatively known as Birds of Paradise or Astrapias.)

FAMILY/GENUS	SPECIES/SUBSPECIES	ENGLISH NAMES
Astrapia	*mayeri*	Ribbon-tailed Astrapia
		Wire-tailed Bird of Paradise
		Shaw-Mayer's Ribbon-tailed Bird of Paradise
	rothschildi	Huon Astrapia
		Lord Rothschild's Bird of Paradise

(All species of genus *Parotia* alternatively known as Birds of Paradise or Parotias.)

FAMILY/GENUS	SPECIES/SUBSPECIES	ENGLISH NAMES
Parotia	*carolae*	Queen Carola's Parotia

Paradisaeidae Birds of Paradise (cont.)

		Queen Carola of Saxony's Six-plumed Bird of Paradise
	lawesi	Lawes's Six-wired Parotia
		Lawes's Six-plumed Bird of Paradise
	sefilata	Arfak Six-wired Parotia
		Arfak Six-plumed Bird of Paradise
	wahnesi	Wahnes's Six-wired Parotia
		Wahnes's Six-plumed Bird of Paradise
Pteridophora	*alberti*	King of Saxony Bird of Paradise
		Enamelled Bird of Paradise
Cicinnurus	*regius*	King Bird of Paradise
		Little King Bird of Paradise
Diphyllodes	*respublica*	Waigeu Bird of Paradise
		Bare-headed Little King Bird of Paradise
		Wilson's Bird of Paradise
Paradisea	*raggiana*	Red-plumed Bird of Paradise
		Raggiana's Bird of Paradise
		Count Raggi's Bird of Paradise
	guilielmi	Emperor of Germany's Bird of Paradise
		Emperor's Bird of Paradise
		White-plumed Bird of Paradise
	rudolphi	Blue Bird of Paradise
		Prince Rudolph's Blue Bird of Paradise
		Archduke Rudolph's Blue Bird of Paradise
		Prince Rudolph's Bird of Paradise

Corvidae Crows, Magpies, Jays, Ravens

Platysmurus	*leucopterus*	Black-crested Magpie
		Black Magpie★
		Black Jay
Aphelocoma	*ultramarina*	Mexican Jay
		Ultramarine Jay
		Arizona Jay
Cyanolyca	*mirabilis*	White-throated Jay
		Omiltene Jay

FAMILY/GENUS	SPECIES/SUBSPECIES	ENGLISH NAMES
Cissilopha	*beecheii*	Purplish-backed Jay
		Beechey's Jay
	melanocyanea	Bushy-crested Jay
		Hartlaub's Jay
	sanblasiana	Black and Blue Jay
		San Blas Jay
Cyanocorax	*chrysops*	Plush-crested Jay
		Plush-capped Jay
		Pileated Jay
		Pileated Wood Jay
		Blue-naped Jay
		Urraca Jay
	dickeyi	Tufted Jay
		Dickey's Jay
Garrulus	*lanceolatus*	Eurasian Black-throated Jay
		Lanceolated Jay
	lidthi	Lidth's Jay
		Loo-choo Jay
		Ryukyu Jay
Perisoreus	*canadensis*	Grey Jay
		Canada Jay
Urocissa	*erythrorhyncha*	Red-billed Blue Magpie
		Red-billed Magpie
		Red-billed Blue Pie
		Blue Magpie
		Occipital Blue Pie
	flavirostris	Yellow-billed Blue Magpie
		Golden-billed Magpie
Cissa	*chinensis*	Green Magpie
		Hunting Magpie
		Hunting Cissa
Dendrocitta	*formosae*	Grey Treepie
		Himalayan Treepie
		Malaysian Treepie*
	frontalis	Black-browed Treepie
		Collared Treepie
	leucogastra	Southern Treepie
		White-bellied Treepie
	occipitalis	Malaysian Treepie*
		Sumatran Treepie
	vagabunda	Indian Treepie

Corvidae Crows, Magpies, Jays, Ravens (cont.)

		Rufous Treepie
		Wandering Treepie
Crypsirina	*cucullata*	Hooded Racket-tailed Treepie
		Hooded Treepie
		Hooded Magpie
	temia	Bronzed Treepie
		Racket-tailed Treepie
		Black Treepie
Temnurus	*temnurus*	Ratchet-tailed Treepie
		Racket-tailed Treepie [1]
		Notch-tailed Treepie
		Temnurus Magpie

(All species of genera *Podoces* and *Pseudopodoces* alternatively known as Ground Jays or Ground Choughs.)

Podoces	*panderi*	Pander's Ground Jay
		Saxaul Jay
Pyrrhocorax	*graculus*	Alpine Chough
		Yellow-billed Chough
Ptilostomus	*afer*	Piapiac
		Black Magpie*
Corvus	*albicollis*	African White-necked Raven
		Cape Raven
	bennetti	Small-billed Crow
		Little Crow*
	capensis	Black Crow
		Cape Crow
	enca	Little Crow*
		Slender-billed Crow
	kubaryi	Guam Crow
		Mariana Crow
	macrorhynchos	Jungle Crow
		Large-billed Crow
	mellori	South Australian Raven
		Little Raven
	splendens	House Crow
		Indian Crow
	tristis	Grey Crow
		Bare-faced Crow

[1] Unlike the previous species, this bird does not have 'racket-shaped' widened ends to its tail feathers, but has notches along the tail like a ratchet.

Appendix

This appendix contains the English names which have been shown in the main list, but which are misleadingly used for more than one species of bird. These English names appear in the main list at least once, but not necessarily more than once, because some of the other species to which these names apply do not have an alternative name. Similarly, not all the scientific names listed here are in the main list; those which are not included are marked †.

ENGLISH NAMES	SCIENTIFIC NAMES	PAGE
Alder Flycatcher	*Empidonax alnorum*	106
	Empidonax traillii	107
Alexandrine Parrot	*Polytelis alexandrae*	65
	Psittacula eupatria eupatria	70
Banded Quail	*Rhynchortyx cinctus*	35
	Philortyx fasciatus†	
Bare-eyed Partridge		
Bronze-winged Pigeon	*Petrophassa scripta*	52
	Petrophassa smithii	52
Bare-throated Tree Partridge	*Arborophila brunneopectus*	36
	Arborophila javanica	37
Black and Orange Flycatcher	*Ficedula mugimaki*	137
	Ficedula nigroufa	137
Black-crowned Bush Shrike	*Tchagra australis*	118
	Tchagra senegala	118
Black Cuckoo Shrike	*Campephaga phoenicea*	113
	Campephaga flava†	
Black-faced Lovebird	*Agapornis nigrigenis*	68
	Agapornis personata	69
Black-fronted Bush Shrike	*Malaconotus multicolor*	118
	Malaconotus nigrifrons†	
Black-headed Greenfinch	*Carduelis ambigua*	160
	Carduelis spinoides	160

ENGLISH NAMES	SCIENTIFIC NAMES	PAGE
Black-headed Hawfinch	*Coccothraustes migratorius*	162
	Coccothraustes personatus	162
Black-headed Sibia	*Heterophasia capistrata*	130
	Heterophasia melanoleuca	130
Black-headed Siskin	*Carduelis magellanicus*	160
	Carduelis notatus†	
Black-headed Weaver	*Ploceus cucullatus*	174
	Ploceus melanocephalus	174
Black Imperial Pigeon	*Ducula melanochroa*	57
	Ducula whartoni	57
Black Magpie	*Platysmurus leucopterus*	184
	Ptilostomus afer	186
Black Robin	*Saxicoloides fulicata*	122
	Turdus nigriceps	124
	Petroica traversi	138
Black-shouldered Kite	*Elanus caeruleus*	28
	Elanus notatus†	
	(confined to Australia)	
Black-throated Babbler	*Stachyris nigriceps*	126
	Stachyris nigricollis	126
Blue Crane	*Ardea novaehollandiae*	22
	Egretta sacra	23
	Anthropoides paradisea	39
Blue-eyed Cockatoo	*Cacatua ophthalmica*†	
	Cacatua sanguinea	62
Blue-headed Sunbird	*Nectarinia alinae*†	
	Nectarinia bannermani	143
Blue-headed Tanager	*Tangara cyanicollis*	154
	Tangara cyanocephala	154
Blue Quail	*Callipepla squamata*	34
	Coturnix adansonii†	
Blue-winged Pitta	*Pitta brachyura*	104
	Pitta moluccensis	104
Cape Canary	*Serinus canicollis*	159
	Serinus totta totta	160
Celebes Hornbill	*Penelopides exarhatus*	94
	Aceros cassidix	94
Chestnut-breasted Bunting	*Emberiza stewarti*	147
	Emberiza tahapisi	147
Chestnut Seedeater	*Sporophila castaneiventris*	149
	Sporophila cinnamomea†	

ENGLISH NAMES	SCIENTIFIC NAMES	PAGE
Collared Seedeater	*Sporophila collaris*	149
	Sporophila torqueola	149
Common Bunting	*Emberiza calandra*	146
	Emberiza citrinella	146
Common Cowbird	*Molothrus ater*	158
	Molothrus bonariensis	158
Common Waxbill	*Estrilda astrild*	164
	Estrilda troglodytes	165
Crow Pheasant	*Centropus phasianinus*	81
	Centropus sinensis	81
Diablotin	*Pterodroma hasitata*	20
	Steatornis caripensis	83
Dusky Nightjar	*Caprimulgus pectoralis*	84
	Caprimulgus saturatus	84
Dusky Parrot	*Pionus fuscus*	76
	Pionus sordidus	77
Eastern Knot	*Calidris canutus*	45
	Calidris tenuirostris	45
Fairy Tern	*Sterna nereis*	47
	Gygis alba	47
Golden-fronted Parakeet	*Bolborhynchus aurifrons*	74
	Brotogeris chrysopterus tuipara	75
Golden-naped Tanager	*Tangara ruficervix*	155
	Tangara seledon	155
Gorgeous Bush Shrike	*Malaconotus quadricolor*	118
	Malaconotus viridis	119
Great Coucal	*Centropus leucogaster*	81
	Centropus menbeki†	
Greater Golden-backed Woodpecker	*Dinopium javanese*	99
	Chrysocolaptes festivus	101
Greater Pewee	*Contopus fumigatus*	106
	Contopus pertinax	106
Green Barbet	*Meglaima zeylanica*	96
	Buccanodon olivaceum†	
Green Broadbill	*Calyptomena viridis*	102
	Pseudocalyptomena graueri†	
Green Conure	*Aratinga leucophthalmus*	72
	Aratinga holochlora holochlora†	
Green Coucal	*Ceuthmochares aereus*	81
	Centropus viridis	81

ENGLISH NAMES	SCIENTIFIC NAMES	PAGE
Green Hanging Parrot	*Loriculus exilis*	69
	Loriculus vernalis	70
Green Woodpecker	*Piculus rubiginosus*	99
	(New World species)	
	Picus viridis†	
	(Eurasian species)	
Grenadier Waxbill	*Uraeginthus granatina*	164
	Uraeginthus ianthinogaster	164
Grey-faced Tit-Babbler	*Macronous flavicollis*	127
	Macronous kelleyi	127
Grey-headed Parakeet	*Psittacula caniceps*	70
	Psittacula himalayana	70
Grey-headed Silverbill	*Lonchura caniceps*	169
	Lonchura griseicapilla	169
Grey Tit	*Parus afer*	140
	Parus major	140
Grey Waxbill	*Estrilda caerulescens*	165
	Estrilda troglodytes	165
Grey-winged Francolin	*Francolinus afer*	35
	Francolinus africanus†	
Grey Wood Pigeon	*Columba argentina*	48
	Columba unicincta	49
Groove-billed Barbet	*Lybius bidentatus*	97
	Lybius dubius	97
Grosbeak Weaver	*Neospiza concolor*	160
	Amblyospiza albifrons†	
Half-moon Conure	*Aratinga aurea*	72
	Aratinga canicularis	72
Harlequin Quail	*Coturnix delegorguei†*	
	(Confined to Africa)	
	Cyrtonix montezumae mearns	35
	(New World species)	
Hodgson's Pipit	*Anthus hodgsoni*	112
	Anthus roseatus	112
Hooded Siskin	*Carduelis cucullatus*	160
	Carduelis magellanicus	160
Imperial Fruit Pigeon	*Ducula aenea*	56
	Ducula concinna	57
Indian Mynah	*Acridotheres ginginianus*	180
	Acridotheres tristis	180
Island Imperial Pigeon	*Ducula myristicivora*	57
	Ducula pistrinaria	57

ENGLISH NAMES	SCIENTIFIC NAMES	PAGE
King Parrot	*Eclectus roratus roratus*	64
	Alisterus scapularis	65
	Purpureicephalus spurius	65
King Vulture	*Sarcogyps calvus*	29
	(Asiatic species)	
	Sarcorhamphus papa†	
	(New World species)	
Lavender Waxbill	*Estrilda caerulescens*	165
	Estrilda perreini	165
Little Button Quail	*Turnix sylvatica*	38
	Turnix velox	38
Little Crow	*Corvus bennetti*	186
	Corvus enca	186
Little Saffron Finch	*Sicalis columbiana*	148
	Sicalis luteola	149
Little Weaver	*Ploceus luteolus*	174
	(English name often	
	transposed with Slender-	
	billed Weaver.)	
	Ploceus pelzelni	175
Long-tailed Wren Babbler	*Spelaeornis chocolatinus*	126
	Spelaeornis longicaudatus	126
Malaysian Treepie	*Dendrocitta formosae*	185
	Dendrocitta occipitalis	185
Masked Tanager	*Tangara larvata*	154
	(Sometimes shown as	
	subspecies of *nigrocincta*.)	
	Tangara nigrocincta	154
Mountain Bulbul	*Hypsipetes mcclellandii*	117
	Andropadus montanus†	
Mountain Canary	*Serinus alario*	158
	Carduelis uropygialis	160
Mountain Finch	*Serinus citrinella*	159
	Emblema picta	166
Noisy Friarbird	*Philemon buceroides*	145
	Philemon corniculutus	145
Olive-backed Sunbird	*Nectarinia jugularis*	143
	Nectarinia verticalis	144
Orange-tufted Sunbird	*Nectarinia bouvieri*†	
	Nectarinia osea	143
Ovenbird	*Furnarius rufus*	102
	Seiurus aurocapillus†	

ENGLISH NAMES	SCIENTIFIC NAMES	PAGE
Painted Bunting	*Passerina ciris*	151
	Passerina versicolor	151
Painted Finch	*Emblema picta*	166
	Chloebia gouldiae	168
Painted Francolin	*Francolinus picta*	36
	Francolinus rufopictus	36
Pale-headed Mannikin	*Lonchura maja*	169
	Lonchura pallida	170
Pearl-headed Silverbill	*Lonchura caniceps*	169
	Lonchura griseicapilla	169
Pied Babbler	*Turdoides bicolor*	127
	Turdoides hypoleucus	127
Plaintive Cuckoo	*Cuculus merulinus†*	
	Cacomantis merulinus	80
Purple Gallinule	*Porphyrula alleni*	42
	(Old World species)	
	Porphyrula martinica†	
	(New World species)	
Purple-headed Glossy Starling	*Lamprotornis purpureiceps*	178
	Lamprotornis purpureus	178
Red-bellied Tit	*Parus davidi*	140
	Parus rubidiventris	140
Red-capped Parrot	*Purpureicephalus spurius*	65
	Pionopsitta pileata	76
Red-crowned Parrot	*Cyanoramphus novaezelandiae*	67
	Poicephalus gulielmi	68
	Amazona viridigenalis	78
Red-headed Parrot Finch	*Erythrura cyanovirens*	167
	Erythrura psittacae	168
Red-headed Weaver	*Quelea erythrops*	175
	Malimbus rubriceps†	
Red-throated Lorikeet	*Charmosyna amabilis†*	
	Charmosyna rubrigularis	60
Red-winged Parrotlet	*Touit dilectissima dilectissima*	75
	Touit heutii	75
Rock Bunting	*Emberiza cia*	146
	Emberiza tahapisi	147
Ruppell's Weaver	*Ploceus velatus*	175
	Ploceus galbula†	
Scaly-fronted Weaver	*Sporopipes frontalis*	173
	Sporopipes squamifrons	173

ENGLISH NAMES	SCIENTIFIC NAMES	PAGE
Scarlet-tufted Malachite	*Nectarinia johannae*	143
Sunbird	*Nectarinia johnstoni*	143
Slender-billed Weaver	*Ploceus luteolus*	174
	Ploceus pelzelni	175
Snake Eagle	*Circaetus cinerus*	29
	Circaetus gallicus	29
Song Sparrow	*Zonotrichia capensis*	147
	Zonotrichia leucophrys	147
Spectacled Barwing	*Actinodura egertoni*	129
	Actinodura ramsayi	129
Spectacled Weaver	*Ploceus nigricollis*	175
	Ploceus ocularis†	
Steel Finch	*Vidua chalybeata*	172
	Vidua funerea	172
Streaked Laughing Thrush	*Garrulax virgatus*	128
	Garrulax lineatus†	
Sula Starling	*Basilornis galeatus*	180
	Streptocitta albertinae	180
Three-coloured Parrot Finch	*Erythrura trichroa*	168
	Erythrura tricolor	168
Traill's Flycatcher	*Empidonax alnorum*	106
	Empidonax trailii	107
Tri-coloured Parrot Finch	*Erythrura trichroa*	168
	Erythrura tricolor	168
Turquoise Dacnis	*Dacnis cayana*	155
	Dacnis hartlaubi	155
Variable Hawk	*Buteo poecilochrous*	30
	Buteo polyosoma	30
Wallace's Hanging Parrot	*Loriculus amabilis*	69
	Loriculus flosculus	69
White-bellied Martin	*Progne chalybea*	111
	Progne dominicensis	111
White-tailed Nightjar	*Caprimulgus cayennensis*	84
	Caprimulgus pectoralis	84
White-winged Black Tit	*Parus leucomelas*	140
	Parus nuchalis	140
Wood Ibis	*Mycteria americana* (New World species)	23
	Ibis ibis (Old World species)	23
Yellow-backed Weaver	*Ploceus dichrocephalus*	174
	Ploceus melanocephalus	174

ENGLISH NAMES	SCIENTIFIC NAMES	PAGE
Yellow-billed Grosbeak	*Coccothraustes migratorius*	162
	Coccothraustes personatus	162
Yellow-browed Bunting	*Emberiza chrysophrys*†	
	Emberiza elegans	146
Yellow-crowned Amazon Parrot	*Amazona ochrocephala ochrocephala*	78
	Amazona xanthops	79
Yellow-eyed Junco	*Junco phaenotus*	147
	Junco vulcani	147
Yellow-headed Amazon Parrot	*Amazona ochrocephala ochrocephala*	78
	Amazona ochrocephala oratrix	78
Yellow-vented Bulbul	*Pycnonotus aurigaster*	114
	Pycnonotus goiavier†	
Yellow White-eye	*Zosterops flava*	144
	Zosterops flavifrons	144
	Zosterops lutea	144

Bibliography

AUSTIN, O. L. Jr & SINGER, A. (1962) *Birds of the World*. Hamlyn, London.

BENSON, C. W., BROOKE, R. K., DOWSETT, R. J. & IRWIN, M. P. S. (1971) *The Birds of Zambia*. Collins, London.

BLAKE, E. R. (1953) *Birds of Mexico*. The University of Chicago Press Ltd, London.

BOND, J. (1960) *Birds of the West Indies*. Collins, London.

BRODIE, I. (1986) *Gamebirds of the Northern Hemisphere*. Whitewolf Publications, Aviemore.

BULL, J. & FARRAND, J. (1977) *The Audubon Society Field Guide to North American Birds*. Alfred A. Knopf, New York.

CAMPBELL, B. (1974) *The Dictionary of Birds in Colour*. Michael Joseph Ltd, London.

COLES, D. (1987) *First Breeding Records for Birds Reared to Independence under Controlled Conditions in the United Kingdom*. D. Coles.

DELACOUR, Dr J. (1980) *Wild Pigeons and Doves*. T.H.F., Reigate.

DE SCHAUENSEE, R. M. (1971) *A Guide to the Birds of South America*. Oliver & Boyd, Edinburgh.

FALLA, R. A., SIBSON, R. B. & TURBOTT, E. G. (1960) *A Field Guide to the Birds of New Zealand*. Collins, London.

FORSHAW, J. M. & COOPER, W. (1973) *Parrots of the World*. Doubleday, New York.

GILLIARD, E. T. (1969) *Birds of Paradise and Bowerbirds*. Weidenfeld & Nicolson, London.

GOODERS, J. ed. (1969–1971) *Birds of the World*. IPC Magazines Ltd, London.

GRUSON, E. S. (1976) *A Checklist of the Birds of the World*. Collins, London.

BIBLIOGRAPHY

HANZAK, J. (1965) *The Pictorial Encyclopedia of Birds*. Hamlyn, London.

HARRISON, DR C. J. O. (1982) *An Atlas of Birds of the Western Palaearctic*. Collins, London.

IMMELMANN (1965) *Australian Finches*. Angus & Robertson (Publishers) Pty Ltd, Sydney.

KING, B., WOODCOCK, M. W. & DICKINSON, E. C. (1976) *A Field Guide to the Birds of South East Asia*. Collins, London.

LANSDOWNE, J. F. & LIVINGSTONE, J. A. (1966) *Birds of the Northern Forest*. McClelland & Stewart Ltd, Toronto.

MARTIN, R. M. (1983) *The Dictionary of Aviculture*. B. T. Batsford Ltd, London.

MEE, A. (c. 1930) *I See All – The World's First Picture Encyclopedia*. The Amalgamated Press, London.

NEWMAN, K. (1983) *Birds of Southern Africa*. Macmillan South Africa (Publishers) Pty Ltd.

PETERSON, R. T. (1961) *A Field Guide to Western Birds*. Houghton, Mifflin Company, Boston.

RESTALL, R. L. (1975) *Finches and Other Seed Eating Birds*. Faber & Faber, London.

RISDEN, D. H. S. (1953) *Foreign Birds for Beginners*. Iliffe, London.

ROBBINS, G. E. S. (1984) *Partridges*. Boydell Press, Woodbridge.

ROGERS, C. R. (1954) *Foreign Birds*. W. & G. Foyle Ltd, London.

RUTGERS, A. (1965) *The Handbook of Foreign Birds*. Blandford Press, London.

RUTGERS, A. & NORRIS, K. A. (1977) *Encyclopedia of Aviculture*. Blandford, Poole.

SERLE, W., MOREL, G. J. & HARTWIG, W. (1977) *A Field Guide to the Birds of West Africa*. Collins, London.

SLATER, P. A. (1975) *A Field Guide to Australian Birds – Passerines*. Scottish Academic Press, Edinburgh.

SMITH, G. A. (1979) *Lovebirds and Related Parrots*. Paul Elak Ltd, London.

SOOTHILL, E. & WHITEHEAD, P. (1978) *Wildfowl of the World*. Blandford, Poole.

TUCK, G. & HEINZEL, H. (1979) *A Field Guide to the Seabirds of Southern Africa and the World*. Collins, London.

WALTERS, M. (1980) *The Complete Birds of the World*. David & Charles, North Pomfret (Vermont), Newton Abbot and London.

WAYRE, P. (1969) *A Guide to the Pheasants of the World*. Country Life Books, London.

WHISTLER, H. (1935) *Popular Handbook of Indian Birds*. Gurney & Jackson, London.

WILLIAMS, J. G. (1963) *A Field Guide to the Birds of East and Central Africa*. Collins, London.

WOODCOCK, M. (1980) *Collins' Handguide to the Birds of the Indian Sub-Continent*. Collins, London.

Index

English Names

Accentors 120
Akalats 120–1, 124
Albatrosses 19
Amadinas 171
Amazillas 87
Amazon Parrots 77–9
Anhingas 22
Ant-pittas 103–4
Ant-shrikes 103
Ant-thrushes 103–4
Ant-vireos 103
Ant-wrens 103
Antbirds 103–4
Apalis 135
Aracaris 97–8
Argus 38
Astrapias 183
Atlapetes 150
Attila 106
Auks 47–8
Automolus 102–3
Avadavats 165–6
Avocet 45
Avocetbill 89
Azurecrown 87

Babax 127
Babblers 124–30
Bald Crow 130
Barbets 95–7
Barbthroats 85
Barwings 129
Batis 138
Bazas 28
Bearded Tit 131
Becards 109
Bee-eaters 93
Bellbirds 110

Berry-eaters 109
Bicheno 167
Bigua 22
Birds of Paradise 182–4
Bishops 176–7
Bitterns 23
Blackbirds 157
Blackcock 33
Blue-bills 163
Blue-tails 121
Blue Wrens 135–6
Bluebird 117
Bobwhite 34
Bonxie 46
Boobies 21
Boubou 118
Bowerbirds 182
Brainfever Bird 80
Brambling 158
Brilliants 88
Broadbills 101–2
Bronzewing 52
Budgerigar 67
Bulbuls 114–17
Bullfinches 150, 161–2
Buntings 146–8, 151
Bush Chats 120–2
Bush Larks 110
Bush Robins 120–1
Bush Shrikes 118–19
Bush Warblers 135
Bustard Quails 38
Bustards 42–3
Butcherbirds 182
Button Quails 38
Buzzards 28–30

Caciques 156

Cahow 20
Caiques 76, 79
Calfbird 110
Calornis 177
Camaroptera 135
Canaries 158–60
Capuchinbird 110
Caracaras 31
Cardinals 150–1
Cariamas 42
Carib 86
Cassowaries 17
Catbird 120, 182
Chachalacas 32
Chaffinches 158
Chat Tyrants 105
Chats 120–2
Chatterers 109, 127
Chickadees 141
Chlorophonia 154
Chloropsis 117
Chorunda 34
Choughs 186
Chukar 35
Cicada Bird 113
Cissa 185
Cisticolas 134–5
Cockatiel 62
Cockatoos 60–2
Cocks-of-the-Rock 108–9
Colies 90
Combassou 172
Comet 89
Conures 72–4
Cookacheea 84
Coot 42
Coppersmith 96
Coquettes 86

Cordon-Bleus 164
Corellas 62
Cormorants 21-2
Corncrake 41
Cotingas 109
Coua 81
Coucals 81
Coural 93
Courlon 39
Coursers 46
Cowbirds 158
Crakes 40-1
Cranes 23, 39
Creepers 102
Crested Babblers 131
Crimson-wings 163
Crocodile Bird 46
Crossbills 161
Crow Pheasant 81
Crows 186
Crow Tit 132
Cuckoo Doves 51
Cuckoo Shrikes 113
Cuckoos 80-1
Curlews 44
Currasows 32-3
Cut-throat 171

Dabchicks 19
Dacnis 155
Darters 22
Diablotin 20, 83
Diglossas 156
Dikkop 45
Diochs 175
Dipper 119
Divers 19
Dollarbird 94
Dotterels 43-4
Dovekie 47
Doves 49-56
Dowitchers 44
Drongos 181-2
Ducks 25-8
Dunnock 120
Dyal Bird 121

Eagles 28-31
Egrets 22-3

Eiders 27
Elaenias 107
Emeralds 86-7
Eremomelas 135
Euphonias 153-4

Falconets 31
Falcons 31
Fantail 138
Fig Parrots 62-3
Finch Larks 110
Finches
  Emberizidae 148-50
  Estrildidae 162-72
  Fringillidae 158-61
Fire-tailed Finches 166
Firecrown 88
Firefinches 163-4
Firethroat 121
Flame-bearer 90
Flamingos 24
Flatbills 107
Flickers 99
Floricans 43
Flower-peckers 131,
  141-2
Flower-piercers 156
Flufftails 41
Flycatchers
  Muscicapidae 136-9
  Tyrannidae 105-7
Flying Dolphin 88
Fodies 175
Foditany 131
Foliage-gleaners 102-3
Francolins 35-6
Friarbird 145
Fruit-eaters 109
Fruit-suckers 117
Fulmars 19-20
Fulvettas 129-30

Gallinules 42
Gardeners 182
Geese 25, 27-8
Gerygone Warblers 136
Go-Away Birds 79-80
Goldenbacks 99
Goldentails 87

Goldfinch 160
Gonolek 118
Goosander 28
Goshawks 29-30
Gouras 54
Grackles 158, 177, 180
Grass Finches 167
Grassbirds 133
Grassquits 149-50
Grebes 19
Green Bulbuls 114-16
Greenbuls 114-16
Greenfinches 160
Greenshank 44
Grenadiers 164, 176-7
Greybirds 113
Greyhen 33
Greywings 35
Grosbeaks
  Emberizidae 151
  Fringillidae 161-2
  Ploceidae 173
Ground Choughs 186
Ground Hornbills 95
Ground Jays 186
Ground Tyrants 105
Grouse 33
Guans 32-3
Guillemots 47-8
Guinea Fowl 38
Gulls 46-7

Hammerhead Stork 23
Hammerkop 23
Hanging Parrots 69-70
Hangnests 156-7
Harriers 28-9
Hawfinches 162
Hawk Owls 83
Hawks 28-31
Hazel Hen 33
Heath Wren 136
Helmet Shrike 118
Helmetcrest 89
Hemipodes 38-9
Hermits 85
Herons 22-3
Hillstars 88
Hoki 37

Honey-eaters 145
Honeybirds 97
Honeycreepers 155–6
Honeyguides 97
Hornbills 94–5
Horneros 102
Hummingbirds 85–90
Hwa-mei 127

Ibises 23–4
Illadopsis 124
Incas 88
Indigo Bird 172
Ioras 117
Ixulas 131

Jabiru 24
Jacamars 95
Jacanas 43
Jaegers 46
Jay Thrushes 127–8
Jays 184–6
Jeries 126
Jewel-thrushes 104
Johnny Rook 31
Juncos 147
Jungle Fowl 38

Kakariki 67
Kalij 37
Kea 62
Kestrels 31–2
Kingbirds 106
Kingfishers 91–3
Kiskadee 106
Kites 28
Kiwis 17
Knots 45
Kookaburra 92
Korhaans 42–3

Lammergeier 29
Lapwings 43
Larks 110–11
Laughing Jackass 92
Laughing Thrushes 127–8
Leaf-gleaners 102
Leaf-scrapers 102–3
Leafbirds 117

Leatherhead 145
Leiothrix 129
Limpkin 39
Linnet 159
Liocichla 128
Locustbird 178
Loeries 79–80
Longspurs 147
Long-tailed Tits 139
Loons 19
Lories 58–60
Lorikeets 58–60
Lorilets 62
Lotus Bird 43
Lovebirds 68–9
Lowry 66
Lyrebirds 110

Macaws 71–2
Magpies 184–6
Malau Fowl 32
Manakins 108
Mango 86
Mannikins 168–71
Manucodes 183
Manyar 174
Marshbirds 157
Martins 111
Meadowlarks 157
Megapodes 32
Meliphagas 145
Merganser 28
Merlins 31
Metaltails 89
Microecas 138
Miner 145–6
Minivets 113–14
Minlas 129
Mockingbirds 120
Monals 37
Monarch Flycatchers
    138–9
Monjitas 105
Moorhen 41–2
Morepork 83
Motmots 93
Mousebirds 90
Munias 166–71
Murres 47–8

Mynahs 179–81

Native Hen 41
Neddicky 134
Nicators 116
Nighthawks 84
Nightingales 121, 129
Nightjars 84
Niltavas 137
Noddies 47
Nothuras 18
Nuns 168–71
Nuthatches 141

Oilbirds 83
Oldsquaw 28
Olivebacks 162
Olive Weaver 162
Orangethroat 121
Orenpendolas 156
Orioles 156–7, 181
Ovenbirds 102–3
Owlets 83
Owls 81–3
Oxylabes 131

Paddy Bird 171
Parakeets 66–75
Pardalotes 142
Parrot Finches 167–8
Parrotbills 131–2
Parrotlets 74–6
Parrots 62–79
Parson Bird 146
Partridges 35–7
Pastor 179
Peafowl 38
Peewit 43
Pekin Nightingale 129
Pelicans 21
Penduline Tits 140
Penguins 18
Peora 37
Petchery 106
Petrels 19–21
Petronias 173
Pewees 106
Phalaropes 45
Pheasants 37–8

Phoenix 151
Piapiac 186
Picathartes 130
Piculets 99
Pies 185–6
Pigeons 48–57
Pintado 20
Pintail 26
Piopio 139
Pipits 112
Pittas 104–5
Plains Wanderer 39
Plaintain-eaters 79
Plovercrest 86
Plovers 43–6
Plumeleteer 87–8
Plush-capped Finch 150
Pratincole 46
Prinias 133–4
Prions 20
Ptarmigan 33
Puffback Flycatchers 138
Pufflegs 88
Purpletufts 109
Pygmy Parrots 62
Pytilias 162–3

Quail Doves 53–4
Quail Finches 166
Quails 34–6
Quaker Babblers 129–30
Quarrion 62
Quebracho 18
Queleas 175
Quetzals 90

Rails 40–1
Rainbow Bird 93
Ravens 186
Redbreasts 121
Redpolls 160
Redstarts 120–2
Redwing 157
Reedling 131
Rheas 17
Ricebird 171
Riflebird 183
Roadrunner 81
Robin Chats 121

Robins 120–4, 138
Rock Fowl 130
Rock Thrushes 122
Rollers 93–4
Rosefinches 161
Rosellas 66
Rotch 47
Roulroul 37
Rubythroat 121

Sabre-wing 85–6
Saltators 151
Sand Larks 110
Sandgrouse 48
Sandpipers 44–5
Sapphire 87
Saw-wings 112
Scaup 27
Scoters 28
Screamers 24
Scrub-birds 110
Scrub Fowl 32
Scrub Hens 32
Scrub Robins 120
Scrub Wrens 136
Seed-crackers 163
Seedeaters 149, 158–9
Seedsnipe 46
Sericornis 136
Seriemas 42
Serins 158–60
Shags 21–2
Shamas 121–2
Sheartail 89
Shearwaters 19–20
Shelducks 25–6
Shelley 159
Shikra 29
Shoe-bill 23
Short-wing 122
Shovelers 26
Shrike Babblers 129
Shrike Thrushes 139
Shrike Tyrants 105
Shrikes 118–19
Sibias 130
Sicklebill 85, 183
Sierra Finches 148
Silverbills 169–70

Silvereyes 144–5
Siskins 159–60
Siva 129
Skuas 46
Skylark 111
Smew 28
Snipe 44–5
Sora 41
Spadebill 107
Sparrowhawks 29–32
Sparrows
  Emberizidae 147
  Estrildidae 171
  Ploceidae 172–3
Spatuletail 89
Spicebird 171
Spider-hunters 144
Spinetails 84
Spoonbills 24
Spreo 179
Sprosser 121
Spurfowl 36
Stage-maker 182
Starfrontlet 88
Starlings
  Icteridae 157
  Sturnidae 177–81
Starthroat 89
Stilt 45
Stone Curlews 45
Stonechats 122
Storks 23–4
Storm Petrels 21
Sugarbirds 155
Sunangels 88
Sunbeams 88
Sunbirds 142–4
Sungem 89
Swallows 111–12
Swamp Hen 41–2
Swifts 84–5
Sylph 88–9

Tanagers 150–5
Tattler 44
Tchagras 118
Teal 26–7
Temple Bird 171
Ternlet 47

Terns 46–7
Thick-knees 45
Thornbills 136
Thrashers 120
Thrush Nightingale 121
Thrushes 122–4
Tinamous 17–18
Tinkerbirds 97
Tit Babblers 127–30
Titmice 141–2
Tityras 109–10
Todies 93
Tody Flycatchers 107
Tody Tyrants 107
Toucanets 97–8
Toucans 97–8
Towhees 150
Tragopans 37
Tree Babblers 126
Tree-hunters 102
Treepies 185–6
Trillers 113
Trogons 90–1
Tropicbirds 21
Troupial 157
Trumpeters 40
Tui 146

Turacos 79–80
Turnstones 44
Twin-spots 163
Tyrannulets 107–8
Tyrant Flycatchers 105–7
Tyrants 105–6
Tystie 48

Umbrellabird 110

Vanga Shrikes 119
Violet-ear 86
Vultures 29

Wagtails
  Motacillidae 112
  Muscicapidae 138
Waldrap 24
Warblers
  Muscicapidae 132–6
  Sylviinae 132–5
Warbling Finches 148
Waterhens 41–2
Waxbills 162–6
Waxwings 119
Weavers 162–3, 172–7
Wedgebill 89, 102

Whale-headed Stork 23
Wheatears 122
Whimbrel 44
Whip-poor-will 84
Whistlers 139
White-eyes 144–5
Whiteface 136
Whydahs 172–6
Widowbirds 172–6
Wigeon 26
Wood-creepers 102
Wood-hewers 102
Wood Hoopoes 94
Wood Quail 34
Woodnymphs 87
Woodpeckers 99–101
Woodstar 89–90
Wren Babblers 125–6
Wren Warblers 133–6
Wrens 119–20

Xenops 103

Yellow Finches 148
Yellowhammer 146
Yuhinas 131

Zosterops 144–5

Generic Names

Species are alphabetical within the genus. Orders, families and
subfamilies are listed on pages 9–13.

Abeillia 86
Aburria 32
Acanthis 160
Acanthiza 136
Accipiter 29–30
Aceros 94–5
Acridotheres 180
Acrocephalus 133
Actinodura 129
Adamstor 20

Aegintha 165
Aegithalos 139
Aegithina 117
Aegolius 83
Aegypius 29
Aethopyga 144
Afropavo 38
Agapornis 68–9
Agelaius 157
Aglaeactis 88

Aglaiocercus 89
Agriornis 105
Aidemosyne 168
Ailuroedus 182
Aimophila 147–8
Aix 27
Alaemon 110
Alauda 111
Alcedo 91
Alcippe 129–30

Alectoris 35
Alectroenas 56
Alisterus 64–5
Alle 47
Amadina 171
Amandava 165–6
Amaurornis 41
Amazilia 87
Amazona 77–9
Amazonetta 27
Amblyornis 182
Amblyospiza 173
Ammomanes 110
Ampelion 109
Amphispiza 147
Amytornis 135
Anabacerthia 102
Anas 26–7
Andigena 98
Andropadus 114
Anhinga 22
Anisognathus 153
Anodorhynchus 71
Anomalospiza 177
Anous 47
Anser 25
Anthracocerus 95
Anthracothorax 86
Anthreptes 142
Anthropoides 39
Anthus 112
Apalis 135
Apaloderma 91
Aphanotriccus 107
Aphelocephala 136
Aphelocoma 184
Aplonis 177
Aplopelia 51
Aprosmictus 65
Apteryx 17
Apus 84
Aquila 30
Ara 71–2
Aracnothera 144
Aramides 40
Aramus 39
Aratinga 72–3
Arborophila 36–7
Ardea 22

Ardeotis 42
Arenaria 44
Arremonops 150
Astrapia 183
Athene 83
Atlapetes 150
Atrichornis 110
Atthis 90
Atticora 111
Attila 106
Aulacorhynchus 97
Automolus 102–3
Aviceda 28
Aythya 27

Babax 127
Baeopogon 115
Balaeniceps 23
Balearica 39
Bambusicola 37
Barnardius 65–6
Bartramia 44
Basilornis 180
Batis 138
Berenicornis 94
Blythipicus 101
Bolborhynchus 74
Bombycilla 119
Bradornis 136
Bradypterus 132
Branta 25
Brotogeris 75
Bubalornis 172
Bubo 82–3
Bubulcus 22
Buceros 95
Bucorvus 95
Burhinus 45
Busarellus 30
Buteo 30
Buthraupis 153
Butorides 22
Bycanistes 95

Cacatua 61–2
Cacicus 156
Cacomantis 80
Calandrella 111
Calcarius 147

Calicalicus 119
Calidris 45
Callipepla 34
Callocephalon 61
Calochaetes 152
Calyptocichla 115
Calyptomena 104
Calyptorhynchus 61
Camaroptera 135
Campephaga 113
Campethera 99
Camptostoma 107
Campylopterus 85–6
Campylorhynchus 119–20
Capito 95
Caprimulgus 84
Cardinalis 151
Carduelis 160
Cariama 42
Carpococcyx 81
Carpodacus 161
Carpodectes 109
Carpornis 109
Casuarius 17
Catamblyrhynchus 150
Catharus 123
Celeus 99
Centropus 81
Cephalopterus 110
Cepphus 48
Cercococcyx 80
Cercomela 122
Cercotrichas 120
Cereopsis 25
Certhionyx 145
Ceryle 91
Cettia 132
Ceuthmochares 81
Ceyx 91–2
Chaetura 84
Chalcophaps 51–2
Chalcopsitta 58
Chalcostigma 89
Chalybura 87–8
Chamaepetes 32
Charadrius 44
Charmosyna 60
Chauna 24
Chenonetta 27

Cheramoeca 111
Chiroxiphia 108
Chlamydera 182
Chloebia 168
Chloephaga 25
Chlorochrysa 154
Chlorocichla 115
Chloropeta 133
Chlorophanes 155
Chlorophonia 154
Chloropipo 108
Chloropsis 117
Chlorostilbon 86–7
Chrysococcyx 80–1
Chrysocolaptes 101
Chrysomma 127
Chrysuronia 87
Cicinnurus 184
Ciconia 23–4
Cinclus 119
Cinnyricinclus 178
Circaetus 29
Circus 29
Cissa 185
Cissilopha 185
Cisticola 134–5
Cistothorus 120
Cladorhynchus 45
Clamator 80
Clangula 28
Claravis 53
Clytoceyx 92
Cnemophilus 182–3
Coccothraustes 162
Coccyzus 81
Coeligena 88
Coenocorypha 44–5
Colaptes 99
Colibri 86
Colinus 34
Colius 90
Colluricincla 139
Columba 48–9
Columbina 52–3
Contopus 106
Copsychus 121–2
Coracias 93–4
Coracina 113
Coracopsis 68

Corapipo 108
Corvinella 119
Corvus 186
Corythaeola 79
Corythaixoides 79–80
Cossypha 121
Cotinga 109
Coturnicops 41
Coturnix 36
Coua 81
Cracticus 182
Crax 33
Creatophora 178
Creurgops 152
Crex 41
Criniger 116
Crossoptilon 37
Crypsirina 186
Cryptospiza 163
Crypturellus 17–18
Cuculus 80
Cursorius 46
Cyanerpes 156
Cyanochen 25
Cyanolyca 184
Cyanocorax 185
Cyanoliseus 73
Cyanopsitta 71
Cyanoramphus 67
Cyrtonyx 35

Dacelo 92
Dacnis 155
Dactylortyx 35
Damophila 87
Daption 19–20
Daptrius 31
Dendrocitta 185–6
Dendrocolaptes 102
Dendrocygna 25
Dendragapus 33
Deroptyus 79
Dicaeum 141–2
Dicrurus 181–2
Diglossa 156
Dinemellia 172
Dinopium 99
Diomedea 19
Diphyllodes 184

Discosura 86
Dives 157
Drepanornis 183
Dromococcyx 81
Dryocopus 100
Ducula 56–7
Dumetella 120
Dumetia 126
Dysithamnus 103

Eclectus 64
Egretta 22–3
Elaenia 107
Elanus 28
Emberiza 146–7
Emblema 166
Empidonax 106–7
Empidonomus 106
Enicognathus 74
Eolophus 61
Eos 58
Epimachus 183
Eremomela 135
Eremophila 111
Eremopterix 110
Eriocnemis 88
Erythrura 167–8
Esacus 45
Estrilda 164–5
Eubucco 96
Eudromia 18
Eudyptes 18
Eudyptula 18
Eugenes 88
Eulampis 86
Eumomota 93
Eunymphicus 67
Euphonia 153–4
Euplectes 176–7
Eupodotis 42–3
Eurystomus 94
Eutoxeres 85

Falco 31–2
Ficedula 137
Formicarius 103
Forpus 74–5
Foudia 175
Francolinus 35–6

Fringilla 158
Fulica 42
Fulmarus 20
Furnarius 102

Galbula 95
Galerida 111
Gallicolumba 54
Gallinago 44
Gallinula 42
Gallus 38
Gampsorhynchus 129
Garrulax 127–8
Garrulus 185
Gavia 19
Geococcyx 81
Geoffroyus 63
Geopelia 51
Geotrygon 53–4
Geronticus 24
Gerygone 136
Glareola 46
Glaucidium 83
Glaucis 85
Glycichaera 145
Glyphorhynchus 102
Goura 54
Gracula 181
Grallaria 104
Grallaricula 103
Grus 39
Gubernatrix 150
Gygis 47
Gymnophaps 57
Gypaetus 29
Gypohierax 29

Habia 152
Halcyon 92–3
Haliaeetus 28
Hapalopsittaca 76
Harpactes 91
Harpyopsis 30
Heliactin 89
Heliangelus 88
Heliodoxa 88
Heliomaster 89
Hemicircus 101
Henicophaps 52

Heterophasia 130
Hieraaetus 30
Hirundo 112
Hodgsonius 122
Hylacola 136
Hylocharis 87
Hylocryptus 102
Hypargos 163
Hypogramma 142
Hypsipetes 116–17

Ibis 23
Ichthyophaga 28
Icterus 156–7
Ilicura 108
Indicator 97
Iodopleura 109
Irediparra 43
Irena 117
Iridosornis 153
Ixobrychus 23

Jabiru 24
Jabouilleia 125
Junco 147

Ketupa 83
Klais 86
Knipolegus 105

Lagonosticta 163–4
Lagopus 33
Lalage 113
Lampornis 88
Lamprotornis 178
Laniarius 118
Lanius 119
Larus 46–7
Laterallus 41
Legatus 106
Leiothrix 129
Leistes 157
Lepidocolaptes 102
Leptoptilos 24
Leptosittaca 73
Leptosomus 93
Leptotila 53
Lesbia 88–9
Leuconerpes 100

Leucospar 180
Leucosticte 161
Lichmera 145
Limnodromus 44
Liocichla 128
Lioptilus 130
Loboparadisea 182
Locustella 133
Loddigesia 89
Lonchura 168–71
Lophophorus 37
Lophornis 86
Lophortyx 34
Lophospingus 148
Lophostrix 82
Lophura 37
Loriculus 69–70
Lorius 59
Loxia 161
Lurocalis 84
Luscinia 121
Lybius 97
Lycocorax 182
Lyrurus 33

Macgregoria 183
Machetornis 105–6
Macronectes 19
Macronous 127
Macropygia 51
Malaconotus 118
Malacopteron 124–5
Malurus 135
Manacus 108
Mandingoa 163
Manorina 145
Manucodia 183
Megadyptes 18
Megalaima 96
Megalurus 133
Megapodius 32
Meiglyptes 100
Melanerpes 100
Melanitta 28
Melanocorypha 111
Melanotrochilus 86
Melierax 29
Meliphaga 145
Melophus 146

Melopsittacus 67
Melopyrrha 150
Menura 110
Mergus 28
Merops 93
Mesopicos 101
Metallura 89
Metriopelia 53
Micrastur 31
Microeca 138
Microhierax 31
Microparra 43
Micropsitta 62
Microrhopias 103
Microstilbon 90
Milvus 28
Mimus 120
Minla 129
Mino 180
Mirafra 110
Molothrus 158
Momotus 93
Monarcha 139
Monticola 122
Montifringilla 173
Morococcyx 81
Motacilla 112
Muscicapa 137
Muscisaxicola 105
Musophaga 79
Mycteria 23
Myiarchus 106
Myiophoneus 122
Myiopsitta 74
Myiozetetes 106
Myrmecocichla 122
Myrmotherula 103
Myrtis 90

Nandayus 73
Nannopsittaca 75
Napothera 125
Nectarinia 142–4
Nemosia 152
Neochmia 166
Neocichla 178
Neomixis 126
Neophema 67
Neophron 29

Neopsittacus 60
Neospiza 160
Neotis 42
Neoxolmis 105
Nesocharis 162
Nesospiza 148
Nestor 62
Netta 27
Nettapus 27
Nicator 116
Nigrita 162
Niltava 137
Ninox 83
Nothocercus 17
Nothocrax 33
Nothura 18
Numenius 44
Numida 38
Nycticorax 23
Nyctyornis 93
Nymphicus 62

Oceanodroma 21
Ochthoeca 105
Ocyphaps 52
Odontophorus 34
Oena 51
Oenanthe 122
Onycognathus 177
Opisthoprora 89
Opopsitta 62–3
Oreophasis 33
Oreopsittacus 60
Oreortyx 34
Oreotrochilus 88
Oriolus 181
Ornithion 108
Oroaetus 31
Ortalis 32
Ortygospiza 166
Otus 82
Oxylabes 131
Oxypogon 89

Pachycephala 139
Pachyptila 20
Pachyramphus 109
Padda 171
Panterpe 87

Panurus 131
Panyptila 84–5
Paphosia 86
Parabuteo 30
Paradisaea 184
Paradoxornis 131–2
Pardalotus 142
Parmoptila 162
Paroaria 150
Parotias 183–4
Parus 140–1
Passer 172–3
Passerina 151
Pedionomus 39
Pelagodroma 21
Pelecanus 21
Pellorneum 124
Penelope 32
Penelopides 94
Penelopina 32–3
Perdix 36
Pericrocotus 113
Perisoreus 185
Perissocephalus 110
Pernis 28
Petroica 138
Petronia 173
Petrophassa 52
Pezoporus 68
Phaeochroa 85
Phaethon 21
Phaethornis 85
Phalacrocorax 22
Phalaropus 45
Phalcoboenus 31
Phapitreron 54
Phaps 52
Pharomachrus 90
Pheucticus 151
Phigys 59
Philemon 145
Philetairus 172
Philodice 89–90
Philortyx 34
Philydor 102
Phloeoceastes 100
Phoenicopterus 24
Phoeniculus 94
Phrygilus 148

Phyllanthus 130
Phyllastrephus 115–16
Phyllomyias 107
Phylloscopus 133
Picathartes 130
Picoides 100–1
Piculus 99
Picumnus 99
Picus 99
Pinarornis 120
Pinicola 161
Pionites 76
Pionopsitta 76
Pionus 76–7
Pipilo 150
Pipra 108
Pipreola 109
Piprites 108
Pipromorpha 108
Piranga 152
Pirenestes 163
Pitangus 106
Pithys 103
Pitta 104–5
Pityriasis 119
Platalea 24
Platycercus 66
Platyrinchus 107
Platysmurus 184
Plocepasser 172
Ploceus 174–5
Pluvialis 43
Pluvianus 46
Pnoepyga 125
Podiceps 19
Podilymbus 19
Podoces 186
Poephila 167
Pogoniulus 97
Poicephalus 68
Polyboroides 29
Polyborus 31
Polyplectron 38
Polysticta 27
Polytelis 65
Pomatorhinus 125
Poospiza 148
Popelairia 86
Porphyrio 42

Porphyrula 42
Porzana 41
Prinia 133–4
Prioniturus 63
Prionodura 182
Prionops 118
Probosciger 60–1
Procellaria 20
Procelsterna 47
Procnias 110
Prodotiscus 97
Progne 111
Prosopeia 64
Prosthemadera 146
Prunella 120
Psalidoprocne 112
Psarocolius 156
Psephotos 66–7
Pseudeos 58
Pseudoleistes 157
Pseudopodoces 186
Psittacella 63
Psittacula 70–1
Psittaculirostris 63
Psophia 40
Pteridophora 184
Pterocles 48
Pterocnemia 17
Pterodroma 20–1
Pteroglossus 98
Pteronetta 28
Pteruthius 129
Ptilinopus 55–6
Ptilocichla 125
Ptilolaemus 94
Ptiloris 183
Ptilostomus 186
Ptyrticus 124
Puffinus 20
Pulsatrix 83
Purpureicephalus 65
Pycnonotus 114–15
Pygiptila 103
Pygoscelis 18
Pyrocephalus 105
Pyrrhocorax 186
Pyrrhula 161–2
Pyrrhura 73–4
Pytilia 162–3

Quelea 175
Quiscalus 158

Rallina 40
Rallus 40
Ramphastos 98
Ramphocelus 152
Ramphomicron 89
Recurvirostra 45
Remiz 140
Rhamphocoris 111
Rhea 17
Rheinardia 38
Rhinomyias 136–7
Rhipidura 138
Rhodinocicla 152
Rhodopechys 161
Rhodopis 89
Rhodospingus 150
Rhynchocyclus 107
Rhynchortyx 35
Rhynchotus 18
Rimator 125
Riparia 111–12
Rollulus 37
Rostrhamus 28
Rupicola 108–9

Saltator 151
Sapheopico 101
Sappho 89
Sarcogyps 29
Sarcops 181
Sarkidiornis 28
Sarothrura 41
Saurothera 81
Saxicola 122
Saxicoloides 122
Scaphidura 158
Scenopoeetes 182
Schiffornis 108
Schistes 89
Sclerurus 103
Scopus 23
Scotocerca 134
Seicercus 133
Selasphorus 90
Selenidera 98
Semioptera 183

Semnornis 96
Sephanoides 88
Sericornis 136
Sericotes 86
Sericulus 182
Serilophus 102
Serinus 158–60
Setornis 116
Sheppardia 120
Sicalis 148–9
Sitta 141
Smithornis 101–2
Somateria 27
Spelaeornis 125–6
Spermophaga 163
Spheniscus 18
Sphyrapicus 100
Spizaetus 30–1
Spizixos 114
Sporophila 149
Sporopipes 173
Spreo 178–9
Stachyris 126
Steatornis 83
Stelgidopteryx 111
Stephanophorus 153
Stephanoxis 86
Stercorarius 46
Sterna 47
Streptocitta 180
Streptopelia 49–50
Strix 83
Sturnella 157
Sturnus 179–80
Sula 21
Sylvia 133
Sypheotides 43
Syrmaticus 38

Tachyphonus 152
Tadorna 25–6

Tangara 154–5
Tanygnathus 64
Tanysiptera 93
Tauraco 79
Tchagra 118
Teleonema 108
Temnurus 186
Tephrodornis 114
Terpsiphone 139
Tetraophasis 35
Tetrastes 33
Thalurania 87
Thamnistes 103
Thamnophilus 103
Thaumastura 89
Thescelocichla 115
Thinocorus 46
Thraupis 152–3
Threnetes 85
Threskiornis 24
Tiaris 150
Tilmatura 85
Timalia 127
Tinamotis 18
Tinamus 17
Tityra 109–10
Tockus 94
Todirostrum 107
Todus 93
Tolmomyias 107
Touit 75–6
Toxostoma 120
Trachyphonus 97
Tragopan 37
Treron 55
Tribonyx 41
Trichastoma 124
Trichoglossus 58
Tricholimnas 40
Triclaria 79
Tringa 44

Trochocercus 138–9
Troglodytes 120
Trogon 90–1
Tumbezia 105
Turdoides 127
Turdus 123–4
Turnagra 139
Turnix 38
Turtur 51
Tyrannus 106
Tyto 81–2

Uraeginthus 164
Uria 47–8
Urocissa 185

Vanellus 43
Veniliornis 100
Vidua 172
Vini 59–60
Volatinia 149

Wetmorethraupis 153

Xenops 103
Xenornis 103
Xenospiza 147
Xenotriccus 107
Xiphocolaptes 102
Xipholena 109
Xiphorhynchus 102
Xolmis 105

Yuhina 131

Zenaida 52
Zonotrichia 147
Zoothera 122–3
Zosterops 144–5